MISSIONARIES, MERCENARIES AND MISFITS

Russell and Patricia Wolford

An American Family Living in the Third World

It's better to dare mighty things, to win glorious triumphs, even though checkered by failure, than to rank with those poor spirits who neither enjoy much nor suffer much, because they live in that grey twilight that knows neither victory nor defeat.

President Teddy Roosevelt

Missionaries, Mercenaries and Misfits

ISBN 978-1622873-44-9 PRINT
ISBN 978-1622-873-43-2 EBOOK

LCCN 2013950302

September 2013

Distributed by
First Edition Design Publishing, Inc.
P.O. Box 20217, Sarasota, FL 34276-3217
www.firsteditiondesignpublishing.com

Father's Press
Lee's Summit, MO
www.fatherspress.com

TABLE OF CONTENTS

ACKNOWLEDGEMENTS

A few years before my mother died, she asked me to sit with her and talk. There was a lull in the conversation, so I said, "I want to write a book." At the time, I had no idea of writing a book or even what I would write about. It wasn't until twenty years later that Mike Smitley of Father's Press, accepted our manuscript, and that dream became a reality. So, this book is in honor of Virginia Feustel Linthicum.

We want to thank the people, friends and strangers, who have helped and believed in us. Many years ago, before we wrote this book, Beatty Lightle met with us in cafes and discussed our "writings" as well as encouraged each other. Then Kendra Griffin, a friend of Laura, our oldest daughter, took the time and patience to draw us out a little more in our story telling of our first attempts. Thank you to Ned Johnston for offering to read the book through and give us his thoughts. Sharon Roberts, a published Christian author, also believed in us and said we would get our book published. She had been praying about it, along with our Ladies Bible Study group.

And then there were strangers who encouraged us without knowing it. The lady at the book fair who was selling her book and said she simply sent a letter to a publisher and they picked it up. So Russ sent a letter to Father's Press and they picked it up. Lastly, while talking Conversational English with one of my students at a French Café, a lady sitting nearby overheard Russ tell one of his African stories. She moved her chair closer and wanted to hear the ending of the story, and said, "You should write a book!"

We want to thank our children who shared the adventures and caught the spirit of living in the Third World.

Patricia Linthicum Wolford

FOREWORD

In 1986, Mogadishu, Somalia, was the safest capital in Africa. The people were nomads and their world view was different than that of Westerners. Somalia was an isolated and unique place. It was partitioned by the colonial powers of England, Italy and France. This partition remains a sore spot with Somalis. Many pan-Somalists want to unify Southern Somalia, Somaliland in the north, Djibouti, northeastern Kenya and the Ogaden region of Ethiopia. Mogadishu was where we were introduced to the Third World and where our adventure began. Mogadishu was peaceful, so we didn't worry about crime and the usual petty thievery of most African cities. Our biggest concerns centered on not getting sick, how to beat the heat and where to get a good meal. We learned to cope in an alien environment, and it was exciting.

The motto of Papua New Guinea was "Expect the Unexpected". Beauty and danger existed in a strange harmony like nowhere else. The rugged terrain was punctuated by rushing rivers and plunging ravines. Some of the tribes remained isolated and primitive. Offshore, the waters of the Pacific Ocean varied in beautiful shades of green and aquamarine. There were many idyllic places to visit, but Port Moresby, the capital, was one of the most dangerous places on earth. Building houses in a squatter settlement among rascals, thieves and tribal wars was exciting, scary and fulfilling. The lessons learned in Port Moresby were helpful in our return to East Africa.

A return to Somalia in 1994 was vastly different than our introduction to Somalia in the previous decade. A civil war had broken out, and Somalia was in chaos. Much of the time on a project site in southern Somalia was filled with routine relief work, but an ominous feeling always filled the air. The quiet could easily be broken and a crisis could quickly arise at any moment. This was necessarily a time of negotiating with clan leaders and dealing with clan militia. In addition, living in Nairobi, Kenya and working with street kids and dealing with the dangers they faced was an occupation in itself.

The authors, Russell and Patricia, had different experiences and individually they participated in different events. Furthermore, when they experienced the same thing, they often viewed it differently. As a result this story is told in two voices.

PART I
MOGADISHU, SOMALIA
1986-1988

ARRIVAL IN MOGADISHU

Russ

As the Somali Airways 707 circled on its approach to Mogadishu International, we had a bird's eye view of Mogadishu. Mogadishu was a city of Arab and Italian influence, with whitewashed and pastel walls, ancient mosques, statues of heroes on horses, and a statue of a boy throwing a stone. From the air it looked like a movie set or even a caricature of an ancient, exotic, remote city of lore. The pale walls and minarets set like citadels on the Indian Ocean. Other expatriates had their own way of describing Mogadishu; our neighbor said it was like going to the moon.

When the time came for an overseas assignment with USAID (United States Agency for International Development), Somalia was one of the available posts. It was about this time that I read a travel article, Perfecting the Mogadishu Saunter, by Blaine Harden of the Washington Post, which highlighted the pleasures and intrigue of Somalia's capital city. This heightened my interest in the exotic country on the Horn of Africa, so I lobbied for the posting to Somalia. It was also a "make or break" situation with regard to the bureaucratic pitfalls that were awaiting me.

I would be the first full-time Contracting Officer and thought it would be a great opportunity. Most of the work at this time was economic development centered around making hard currency available in the country for businessmen, as well as military assistance to America's new allies on the Horn of Africa.

Pat, my wife, who was six months pregnant, was very excited to be going overseas again. She hoped to get to know the people and experience a different culture. Pat wanted to be around people from different countries. At this time Somalia was a quiet country that few people knew about, and family and friends had to look at a map to see where it was. Some even had a hard time pronouncing Mogadishu.

En route to Somalia, I was able to show Paris, France to the family that included Laura, age 8 and Katie, age 2. On a previous visit to the most romantic city in the world, I remembered sitting at a quaint sidewalk café. Street lights framed the wide boulevards and the arching bridges. The silhouette of the illuminated Eiffel Tower reflected off the Seine River. I thought that Pat and the kids would certainly like to see this place.

Their impression of the city, however, wasn't quite what I expected. Their remembrance of Paris was me saying, "It's just one more bridge, just one more bridge to go." I had a hard time finding the places that I wanted to show the family. We did find the souvenir stands. Pat wanted to buy a trinket for Laura. She found a pen with a picture of the Eiffel Tower on one side. Laura was very pleased. Pat was too, until she turned the pen around and there was a picture of a woman with her bosoms showing. We kept it for many years. Our second daughter, Katie, was young and hard to handle on the long walks on the city streets. Also, Pat was pregnant. We stayed at Hotel Brighton across from The Tuileries Garden. The hotel had French doors from floor to ceiling and a deep bathtub. What to eat was the challenge every day. Not knowing French, we weren't sure of what we were ordering or how much it cost, so we drank hot chocolate and ate baguettes. To my surprise everyone was anxious to get going and move on to our next stop, Nairobi, Kenya.

In Nairobi we stayed at the Jacaranda Hotel, a mid-range, locally owned hotel that was very comfortable. It had a swimming pool, beautiful bougainvillea flowers and included a mix of tourists and local guests. Sitting around the pool, the aroma of tropical flowers mixed with the scent of "nama choma" (grilled meat) wafting from the open grills next to the kitchen. Across the side street from the hotel was the Pizza Garden, which at a later time would be our favorite pizza joint.

We arrived in Nairobi just in time to celebrate my 39th birthday at the Nairobi Game Park. This was "big sky" country. The horizon was distant and the reach of the savannahs seemed limitless. The blues in the sky had a variety of shades and richness similar to that of the multitude of greens in the coral atolls of the South Pacific.

At a stop at a picnic area where we could get out of the tour van, we took a walk along a path and ran into a troop of baboons. Pat wanted to walk right past them, but I thought they were too unpredictable and could be dangerous. I insisted that we turn around. Pat and the girls called me a chicken, but I got the last laugh. A group of little vervet monkeys were loitering around the parking area, so Pat walked over to them to play. We soon heard a scream, and she came running toward the van with a gang of little monkeys nipping at her heels. I think it was Elspeth Huxley who said that animals were the soul of Africa. This may be true, but while living in Somalia, our experiences were with baboons and warthogs rather that with the more majestic beasts of the continent. Lions and elephants would have to wait. Now we were going to Mogadishu, an hour's flight from Nairobi, but a world away.

As we circled Mogadishu prior to landing, everything looked white. White-washed buildings and walls were framed against a sweeping coast line. It looked like photos from National Geographic. The air-conditioning was turned off in the plane as we got ready to disembark, and it was getting warmer and warmer. Pat carefully set the girls' hats on their heads, just as her mother had done for her when arriving in a new country many years ago. The hats promptly blew off as we alighted from the plane. Instead of arriving poised and confident, we were hot, bedraggled and irritable. We all wondered what on earth we were doing here.

Getting through the purgatory of the Mogadishu airport was a trial for the spirit. Arriving passengers were herded into an area half the size of a tennis court and the doors locked behind them. We couldn't go back, and the customs desk loomed ahead like a mountain to be climbed. Once inside the airport building, there was confusion as we followed a wave of people, all filling out a myriad of forms in duplicate. A soothing breeze abruptly stopped as the airport guards locked the doors behind us. The pink walls inside were painted with pictures of Somalis serving their country and local market scenes. Katie swung on poles to kill the time. After surviving the stifling heat and the jet exhaust fumes that were seeping into the building, our passports were stamped, and the battle for the baggage began. This airport did not have a baggage carousel. The luggage was on a shelf behind a counter, and the guys behind the counter handed out bags as people screamed and pointed at their piece of luggage.

It was finally a relief to step outside and see a friendly American face. "Did you make it through alright?" asked the smiling American face, as we were standing outside of the Mogadishu airport. "That was quite an experience." Pat said as she wiped the perspiration from her face and watched with one eye as sixteen pieces of luggage were lifted into a van.

MOGADISHU BEFORE THE WAR

RUSS IN D.C. USAID OFFICE

LIVING IN MOGADISHU

Pat

It took quite a bit of effort to get accustomed to Mogadishu. Just about every capital city in the world has someplace, a little corner, a neighborhood or something, where it is possible to get a fix of Western culture. Not so in Mogadishu. Everything in Mogadishu was exotic to the expatriate. Even the American Club seldom had Coca Cola, just fresh mango juice. Many Americans maintained their sense of identity by playing softball on the weekends. The imported feel of Americana was accentuated by the lawn chairs and beer coolers. Out on the street that feeling of familiarity evaporated with the smell of incense and cow dung, and the sight of donkey carts, goats and camels in the middle of the road. The feeling of being in a new and exotic place was accented by the daily, mournful prayer calls.

We woke at 6:00 a.m., before the heat became too oppressive. Every day in Mogadishu was scorching hot. The equatorial sun seared Somalia relentlessly. It was dustier than we could have imagined, but the wind blew mercifully from the ocean and brought some measure of relief. The white dust often swirled up into the air and looked like snow as it fell back to the parched earth.

Looking from the second story balcony of our new house, the blue-green Indian Ocean could be spotted over the sea of red tile roofs. I had to think where I was for a minute as I gazed down at our sandy courtyard, which connected the other three houses of our compound. The white-washed walls and ancient mosques had a sparse and intense beauty.

Our house was a big, two storey, with access to a flat roof. The furniture was Queen Anne, and the drapes were hand sewn by Somalis. Each room had an air conditioner. We were living in a compound with four other American families in four white houses, with a sandy courtyard between us. There was no grass, trees, statues or fountains in the courtyard. A swing set stood alone, swinging in the breeze and hot sun, with no one there. It did have a generator and water storage tank. Sometimes the guards went to the courtyard to chew quat, a mild narcotic that helped them stay awake. The American Embassy had rented this compound from a previous Finance Minister. With Queen Anne furniture, air conditioning in every room, two watchmen and a maid; this hardship post wasn't going to be that much of a hardship, or was it?

From one upstairs window I could look into our Somali neighbor's courtyard where they did all of their cooking in a brick oven. From a different window, I watched the goats file out of an adjacent courtyard and roam down the alley behind our house.

After our effects arrived, Laura and Katie rode their bikes in circles around the house. The entire plot the house sat on was concrete, except for a small area for a garden. Laura, age eight, was traumatized as a result of being pulled away from her familiar home, school and best friend in the States, and then arriving in a place that was incomprehensible. She didn't have her usual bubbly, sunny disposition. The movie tape, Girls Just Want to Have Fun, was played over and over in our house. Katie, at two years, was one ball of speed everywhere. She splashed in the baby pool; played with the other toddlers in our compound; carried her baby dolls; chased after the chickens; pointed to the baboons, and cuddled with the new kitten that Somali neighbors across the alley had given us. Katie had a couple of playmates on the compound. Josh was a little older and lived in the house behind ours. The Allen's had a young daughter in the other house across the courtyard, and the Bond kids next door were just a little older. Laura and Katie pretended that the boxes our effects came in were "their house".

Schooling

We enrolled Laura in The American School of Mogadishu as soon as possible, so she could get acclimated and make some new friends. The school was run by and for Americans, but also included Somali and other expatriate students. School days were Tuesday through Saturday, from 7am-1pm. She made friends and participated in activities such as picnics, baseball games, school festivals and the Girl Scouts. When Laura came home, she would play soccer with the Somali kids across the street from our house.

Katie was enrolled in Bush Babies, a pre-school at the International Club. She learned "Twinkle, Twinkle, Little Star", and other songs from her African teacher.

I began tutoring two Somali children, a first and second grader. They both attended the American School. The second grader was the grandson of President Siad Barre. His father was the Minister of Foreign Affairs. He was bright and curious, but easily distracted. I asked him to write about his favorite things to eat. He mentioned mushrooms, peanut butter and strawberries. "Strawberries! Where do you find strawberries?" I asked. He replied, "My mother brings them from Paris." Apparently each time she had a baby, (six in total), she and the children went to Paris.

I gave the lessons in the air-conditioned storage room. I wasn't sure how much he learned while we froze to death in the storage room. The tutoring was a good experience, and I made $10 an hour.

Every aspect of daily life in Mogadishu was new and untested. One American wife landed in Mogadishu and left the next day. Illness was something everyone lived with throughout their tour. It started for me upon arrival in Somalia, feeling weak and sick. One of the American wives told me to take 7-Up and rest, which did cure the initial queasiness. However, as days passed I learned about giardia and dysentery along with other diseases that people had to live with. It brought utter fatigue and constant sick to the stomach feeling. There was not a day I felt perfectly well. It was amazing how people functioned with constant stomach aches and heat exhaustion. No matter how careful a newcomer was about health issues, the heat was such a good place for bugs to thrive, that people were bound to get some ailment. Most expatriates took malaria pills, so malaria wasn't as big a problem. Stomach issues were often the subject of discussion at expatriate parties. Fortunately the kids did not get sick. I respected the Somalis who had survived in this difficult country.

Somali women seemed to float down the street. Their silky clothing fluttered in the wind. They wore multi-colored sari-type dresses, and covered their shoulders or hair with a "garbasar" or shawl. They chattered away with quick smiles. Their beauty was dazzling; it was difficult to pull your eyes away.

In the evenings we sat on the front porch and watched the sky change color. We waited for the night breeze to come off the ocean. The deep blue sky was contrasted against our white stone wall so beautifully. Clouds formed and floated across the sky from east to west, and as the sun set, the sky took on deeper tones, from pink to purple or from orange to scarlet, until it became ink black.

The same star shone just over our wall each night, sometimes joined by a clear, white moon. At bedtime, Katie said goodnight to the moon, and when there was no moon, she asked where it went. I told her it was at Grandpa's house in Ohio. This was a pleasant time, even if there was turmoil during the day. These times looking at the stars in the black Somali night made a person consider living the rest of their life in Africa. Russ loved sitting on the front porch outside in the night air, listening to the stories of our guards and learning about the clan system.

Watchmen, Clans and Politics

Russ

Our house in Mogadishu was staffed by two watchmen and a maid. The watchmen, Hassan Ali Hassan and Hassan Hussein Handule, were noble and trustworthy characters.

Hassan Ali kept busy during the day working in the garden and cleaning the car. The flower and vegetable seeds that we brought from America didn't produce in the sandy, Somali soil, so Hassan Ali came up with some local plants and seeds that grew well.

I learned a lot about clan politics from Hassan Hussein. Hassan was Dagodi, a Hawiye clan from the Ethiopian border and into northern Kenya. During this time in Somalia, it was taboo to openly discuss clan issues, but I had many such discussions with my Somali friends. Somalis are very fond of politics, and clan issues are the essence of Somali politics.

I found that the Isaaqs, from the northwest, and the Murasade, a small Hawiye clan from around Mogadishu, particularly enjoyed in-depth clan and political discussions. The Abgal, Hassan Ali's clan, which was the largest clan from the Mogadishu area, tended to be reserved and not inclined to get into controversial discussions. The Abgal were unique in their defense of the establishment. Somalis of the other clans took every opportunity to complain about the government and the way the President Siad Barre was manipulating the clans.

One of Barre's more diabolical methods of neutralizing opposition from a particular clan was to jail one of the clan's more respected leaders. In order to win the release of their leader, the rest of the clan would fall in line with Barre's way of thinking. After his release, the prisoner would be given a post in a government ministry, and the opposition would be effectively neutralized. This practice had a long term effect, however, of increasing Barre's paranoia of those even in his government. He steadily withdrew into a cocoon of his own clansmen, who became his sole source of advisors and counsel.

Somali is unique in Africa for its lack of ethnic mix. Other African nations are an amalgamation of various tribes and language groups. All Somalis share the same identity, language, religion and traditions. A basic tenet of all African nations, except Somalia, is the sanctity of the national borders as they currently exist. The regions of Kenya and Ethiopia in which Somalis live, as well as Djibouti, are coveted by pan-Somalists, who yearn to see all Somalis united under one flag.

Shucre

Pat

"Hello Sister." she said. I was meeting Shucre for the first time in order to interview her for the job of "boyessa", a maid. She had worked for the Americans next door, and they recommended her. They were vague, however, about why they let her go.

She had a big, warm smile. Shucre was small, with a slight frame and doe-like eyes, but had a kind of hardness in her face. She was in her thirties, but because Somalis age so fast, she looked older. She said she lived with her mother. I noticed her Somali "dress"- a sheath of fabric worn over her shoulders, sewn on the sides so it billowed in the wind, looked worn with a few tears in it. I noticed her sandals, too, were worn at the heel.

She seemed very eager to work. I offered her the position with the same salary that the other boyessas made, but she asked for more. I gave in a bit and Shucre started working for us the next day. I had some hesitation about getting a maid, but the neighbors seemed to think it was a necessity.

Shucre arrived at 8:00 a.m., cleaned the house, did the laundry and left at 1:00 p.m. I wondered what she would do the next day. She cleaned the house all over again. I asked Sucre to clean the downstairs one day, and the next day to clean the upstairs. She came the next day and cleaned the whole house again. I made a feeble attempt again to explain, but Shucre continued to clean the whole house every day. I let it go but later realized that I should have required her to do the job the way I wanted it done, although it didn't hurt to clean everyday, since the dust accumulated so quickly.

Shucre also baby-sat for us. Katie was excited the first time Shucre showed up at night, but cried when she realized we were leaving. Sucre got out some Somali tapes, and she and Katie danced the night away.

Shucre showed me where to get the material to buy a Somali wrap (the type of dress that Somali women wear). She showed me how to put it on and just laughed as I tucked and pulled to try to keep the thing from falling off. Laura wanted to dress-up too, so Sucre wrapped her in some material, and then went out to show Hassan how she had made a Somali out of Laura. Laura was beginning to bond with Shucre.

Our kitchen was small, narrow and hot without windows, but the wall was made up of beautiful blue Italian tiles. We had to leave the back door open for extra air. It was so hot that once Laura fainted, while I was changing the earrings in her newly pierced ears. The storage room, filled with canned goods and American candy, was next to the kitchen and the coolest room in the house. When the air conditioner was at full speed and the door shut, it was possible to make this room cold.

"No, no, Sister, oven hot!" Sucre exclaimed, as she tried to explain to me what temperature to bake the bread. My attempts at bread-making without a recipe, a mixer or good flour, resulted in something that looked like bread, but tasted like dust.

Sucre was showing me how to make Somali bread. We both wanted the same thing, good bread, but had different ideas on how to get it. She insisted that if the oven was too hot, the bread would burn. I tried to explain that if the oven wasn't hot enough, the bread would stay in too long and be too hard. In spite of our bickering, the bread came out fine, even though the crust was a bit hard, and the inside had a corn-mealy texture. Later I tried the same thing myself, but the dough didn't rise. I just plopped the two loaves together and baked them. Sucre got a big kick out of that.

Russ had a different insight on Sucre. He said she was from the Majerteen tribe, and this was why she was bull-headed and didn't listen. She couldn't help the fact that she got on my nerves. She was Majerteen, and Majerteen are egocentric. The Majerteen think that they are the royalty of Somali clans. To the contrary, many clans have royal family lines and reigning ugas. The best translation for ugas is king. The ugas serves as chief elder of the clan, and for many clans, the title is passed down through family lineage. The Darod clans seem to cling to their tradition of royal lineage more so than other clans. The Majerteen are a sub-clan of the Darod, but they clearly are not the only ones with royal family lines.

Food

Pat

I became proficient at fruit and vegetable shopping in the local markets. The open-air markets were dusty with individual vendors in stalls lined up along a path. Customers shouted a lot as they bargained for the best price. I patronized certain stalls where the vendor was helpful and treated me like the other customers, rather than as an outsider.

We found a bakery that sold fresh bread. It was down a dusty street leading away from the compound, where all sense of familiarity eroded the further away you got from our house. The side streets were nothing more than dirt, goat paths. There was a strong smell of incense and cow dung. Such areas smelled like a stable but with an overhanging mist of incense. This bakery had fresh bread but the rolls always had tiny bugs inside. Initially, we picked them out, but eventually we just ate them without paying much attention.

We also ate a lot of eggs, which were plentiful, like pasta. We had pasta too many times. Now our kids do not like spaghetti. The meat in the local outdoor markets was usually covered with flies. The proprietor would simply shake off the flies and then cut a piece of meat for the customer.

So, we like all Westerners, shopped at the "sanitary meat markets". These were butcher shops that had refrigeration. An Italian grocery at Fiat Circle had imported European goods, such as mozzarella and salami. It was expensive, but a nice treat. We also bought canned food that was available from the embassy commissary. Word got out quickly when new shipments arrived, but the perishables were usually out of date. M&Ms were so popular one had to get there before they were all gone.

I learned a lot about shopping from Shucre. It was an exciting day when she found a source of good, American flour, without bugs. The flour was actually meant for the refugee camps on the Ethiopian border, but was repackaged and sold in the shops here. This was somewhat legitimate since traders from the cities would trade sugar and tea to the refugees for some of their flour and oil rations.

Restaurants

Russ

The first priority after setting up residence in Mogadishu was to find a good place to eat. Mogadishu and southern Somalia were part of Italian Somaliland during the colonial period. The Italian influence remained strong, except the Somalis never took a liking to pizza. Pasta, however, was a big favorite with Somalis, and Mogadishu's coffee bars served excellent cappuccino.

The best dining available was at the three top hotels: Makka; Croce Del Sud, and Gulled. The Makka Hotel was a multi-storied building on a main shopping street called Via Mecca. It was owned by a man named Ali Mahdi, who later became a warlord of the Abgal clan. The Makka dining area was on a terrace with plants and shrubs partitioning the individual tables. One day I took a Somali friend's two boys to the Makka, after we went shopping for a soccer ball. The buffet had a wide variety of vegetables and salads that rivaled an American salad bar. This was a particularly memorable day with two good friends at a pleasant restaurant. On some mornings Pat took the kids to The Makka for breakfast on the veranda, which was cool with beautiful tropical flowers.

We also discovered an outdoor café near our house, at a location called K5. We walked along the dusty road as a family to get the best cappuccino in the world. We think it was due to the freshness of the milk, which often wasn't pasteurized. The patrons in the cafes were men and seldom mixed with foreigners, much less female foreigners. The arrival of Pat and the kids often caused interest and stares, but then they became part of the scenery.

The Croce Del Sud was an old, multi-winged hotel in the center of town, near the Catholic Cathedral. The dining area was in a courtyard, and the setting was exemplary of Mogadishu's characterization as a place lost in time. Balconies surrounded the courtyard, and if it were Argentina rather than Mogadishu, you would expect Eva Peron to come out of her room singing. The white-washed stucco and stray palm or two gave a feeling of being in a movie about some exotic adventure. It was like being transported to an earlier era of the colonial past.

The Gulled Hotel was on the outskirts of town. The accommodations were individual cottages, and the dining hall was a huge, thatched roof, open-air affair. Each of these establishments seemed to have their own particular clientele, but it was generally expatriates and rich Somalis. One thing about the Somalis was that they would host their extended family; however, most Somalis could not afford to eat at the fancy hotels. Often there were no menus, but the waiter would tell you what they had. If the waiter didn't speak English, they would bring someone over who did.

We soon started venturing into what we initially thought to be marginal restaurants and found many of them to be good. Our favorite in this class was the Nile Restaurant with grilled fillet steak and excellent minestrone soup. The Nile was open air seating under a thatched roof.

If it was night, the restaurants were dark because they didn't have electricity to waste, but during the day you had the bright Indian Ocean sunlight. When experimenting with new restaurants, we found that grilled steak and hot soup were safe choices. If we took a liking to a restaurant, we would expand our menu selections, and rarely got sick because of the food we ate. We avoided salad and always ate our meat well-done.

The Mogadishu International Golf and Tennis Club was an expatriate dining and meeting place, known for its cinnamon rolls, goat liver at breakfast and cream caramel for dessert. The cinnamon rolls were either soft or hard, but we ate them either way. This was the only time or place where Pat ate goat's liver. The cream caramel was good and usually had a custard texture and tasted like cream caramel, but at other times it had a firm texture and tasted like cheesecake.

We usually sat outside on the veranda. It was a pleasant, but arid setting with thorn trees, sand and birds chirping. The club was decorated inside with lamps using Somali jugs as shades. The golf course was a mowed pasture with sand putting greens. It wasn't a great course but made a pleasant view from the veranda of the restaurant. There was an Olympic size swimming pool, but was rarely used because of the extreme heat and the lack of shade.

The club was also a social scene for the mothers with young children. The toddler's group met monthly with their toddlers and babies. This was where Pat met mothers from all over the world. She became friends with the English mums. She liked the way the Brits said "Kay tee" for Katie. Pat made play dates with their kids and they introduced Pat to meringues. The British ladies were a breath of fresh air and didn't complain.

All sorts of expatriates relaxed and refreshed themselves on the veranda of the restaurant.

There weren't a whole lot of foreigners living in Mogadishu, so the clientele at the golf club was the same most holiday events. The occasional new face would often be missionaries or development workers on a rest from the bush. One day we met a man we hadn't seen before, sitting alone. He said, "When you first arrive and see a bug in a drink you ordered, you ask for another. Once you have been here a while and you see a bug in the glass, you take the bug out. You've really arrived when you drink the bug and all." He was the first one who mentioned expats as either "missionaries, mercenaries or misfits". He didn't indicate which one he was.

A Baby Shower

I was looking forward to my baby shower at our house. There were many ladies from the toddler group and the International Club. I was happy to have my American friends, my Somalia friends and friends from so many different countries. Our Tonga friend brought her husband, and he seemed to enjoy the festivities as well. I was looking forward to having our baby and never had any doubts or worries about having a new-born while living in Mogadishu. After all, the baby would eventually join the Toddler's Group.

Bush Babies Club at the Mogadishu International Golf and Tennis Club

Mogadishu: Laura and Katie

Laura and Sucre

Mogadishu: Pat in our house

CLANS AND NOMADIC SOCIETIES

Russ

Somalis are descendents of Ham, the second son of Noah, and part of the Cushitic language group. Somalis, as a distinctive ethnic group, are traced to a patriarch called Samaale, around 300 AD. It is not certain if he was Arab or from a Cushitic group. Most likely he was Cushitic, since the Somali language prevailed, rather than Arabic. The subjects of Somali clans and Somali politics as well as historical facts pertaining to Somalia are seldom definitive. Most of the information in this book about such matters was secured through interviews with Somalis. Some of it is information brought to light by people such as I. M. Lewis and Sir Richard Burton.

The patriarchs of the Somali clan system are the Darod, Hawiye and Dir. They arrived on the Horn of Africa around 1200 AD. They were Arabs and brought Islam with them, but they didn't replace the Somali language with Arabic. Clan lineage is a complicated matter. Dir arrived on the Horn of Africa first, followed shortly by Darod and Hawiye. These were the patriarchs of the nomadic clans, known as Samaale.

The agricultural clans of the south are known as Sab. The group that makes up the agricultural clans includes Rahanweyn, Digil and Mirifle. These clans are likely a joining or mixing of the various other Somali clans with coastal people of various origins. In fact, Rahanweyn in one dialect means "people who come together". A detailed illustration of the clan families is included in the Appendix.

Defeating the Colonial Powers

Somalis have always been proficient at repulsing potential invaders. In the 16th Century, the Portuguese, who subjugated Mombasa and colonized Mozambique, bombarded Barawe, a port south of Mogadishu. When they tried to invade Somali territory, they were defeated by Somalia's first national hero, Ahmed Gurey.

Britain established a presence in Somalia in the 19th Century by signing a treaty with the clans of the northwest. British influence inland, however, was thwarted by Sayid Mohamed Abdille Hassan, and his dervishes. During the colonial period, Somalis were not so much ruled by outside powers, as they had special trade relations with the European nations. Somalia was not a place for outsiders to try too hard to exert their influence.

Cultural Differences

The nomadic lifestyle which characterizes all Somalis, even the agriculturalists in the riverine regions of the south who trade camels as well as grow maize, is probably the most striking antithesis to Western culture. The importance of mobility has resulted in Somalis shunning material possessions which serve no life-sustaining purpose. The Somali nomads even carry their houses on the backs of their camels. They have no use for art just for the sake of art; however, many of their functional material possessions are indeed objects of significant artistic value. Some headrests are finely carved but still have a utilitarian purpose. The jugs used to carry milk and water are woven from tree bark, and they take time and talent to make. They look good and are functional.

Woven jugs which are used to transport milk on the backs of camels take several months for the women to make. They are intricate and aesthetically pleasing to the eye. The Somali headrest is a utilitarian item, but many are carved with intricate, undulating plaited designs. The headrest is also a symbol of the herdsman's vigilance. They are not very comfortable to sleep on, but interesting to collect. The jugs and headrests are as much symbols of the Somali nomad as chaps and spurs are a symbol of the American cowboy. Just as spurs are not worn in New York City, headrests were not used in Mogadishu. A trip to the bush was necessary to view the noble, independent Somali nomad living the way that nomads had lived and survived the harsh climate for hundreds of years.

Somalia is an oral society. The Somali language was not written until 1972. All history and traditions have been passed on orally and Somalia's greatest heroes are its poets. The greatest hero-poet was Sayid Mohamed Abdille Hassan. He inspired his allies and riled his enemies with his poetry.

Clan identity is the most important factor in Somali society and politics. Sayid Mohamed Abdille Hassan spoke about clans. He had a lot to say and developed caricatures of the various tribal clans through his poetry. He is most widely known for leading the dervishes against the British. Some clans followed him and some didn't. The decision to join Sayid Mohamed's jihad was much like other political decisions that Somalis will make in the future. What are most important are nationalism or clan interests. Clan interests often trump religion. Compared to the clan and Islam, national interests are of little concern.

Mohamed Hassan said something to the effect that

- the Ogaden will always follow the leader
- the Dublahante will always be the henchmen
- the Isaaq will always kiss the Englishman's ass

Sayid Mohammed probably said these derogatory things about the Isaaq clan, because they allied with the British when he was trying to unite the Somali clans against the colonial powers.

Sayid Mohamed was Ogaden, but he led many of his battles with the British from Las Anod in the territory of his mother's Dublahante clan. The Dublahante and neighboring Warsengeli were not totally behind the Sayid's struggle. Many left northern Somali and moved to areas around Kismayo. These are the people who comprise the Harti clan in that area. The dichotomy between Somali nationalism and clan interests has resulted in many political dilemmas for modern Somalia, from Sayid's Jihad to the union of British and Italian Somaliland after independence, and many issues since.

The Somali Economy

Western donors and relief agencies brought many resources into the country for refugee programs. Furthermore, most of the refugees were ethnic Somalis. Donated flour, rice and vegetable oil was sent to the refugee camps, and the refugees traded some of these foodstuffs for sugar and tea. The traded items were then returned to Mogadishu to be repackaged for sale.

The refugees had been in camps on the Somali side of the Ethiopian border for a decade. The refugees were good for Somalia. Western donors and relief agencies brought resources into the country for refugee programs, not just food but also vehicles and hard currency. Most of the refugees were ethnic Somalis, rather than other tribes from Ethiopia. Donated flour, rice and cooking oil were sent to the camps, and the refugees traded some of these foodstuffs for sugar and tea.

The refugees were in Somalia as a result of the dual calamities in the Ogaden Region of Ethiopia of drought and the 1977-78 border war between Ethiopia and Somalia. The Ogaden has been a contested area since the end of the 19th Century when Menelik II, Emperor of Abyssinia, expanded his empire by taking control of the Ogaden.

In 1935 Mussolini invaded Ethiopia from Somalia, but when the British liberated the area in 1941, the Ogaden was returned to Ethiopia.

Somalia failed to gain ground in the Ogaden in 1961 and 1964 border skirmishes.

The Soviet-trained Somali army invaded Ethiopia in 1977 taking control of most of the Ogaden, but the Soviets backed the new Marxist regime in Addis Ababa. With the Soviet arms and the help of Cuban troops, the Ethiopians drove the Somali army back across the border. This was the last attempt by Somalia to regain the Ogaden.

Somalia's barter economy could be witnessed each day along the Afgoye Road, a major road linking Mogadishu to the town of Afgoye and the agricultural areas along the Shabelli River. In the morning the farmers arrived in Mogadishu with their donkey carts loaded with fodder or charcoal wood. In the late afternoon the donkey carts would flow out of town headed back toward Afgoye with small bags of tea or sugar strapped to the cart.

The population of Mogadishu used a lot of charcoal. Electric power, although unpredictable, was readily available in the city; but 90% of it was used by the expatriates. Most Somalis who had electricity used it only to burn a light bulb. Even the affluent Somalis had the hired help cook in an outdoor cooking area using charcoal.

FRIENDS AND ACTIVITIES

Pat

It was a relief to get away from the constant air-conditioning inside and the frequent sound of a generator outside. I looked forward to visiting our friends who lived closer to the locals and didn't have as many comforts as we. Drannon and Carol Buskirk were here with a contract related to water resources. The Murdocks had worked for Save the Children in the bush on the Shebelle River. When we knew them they lived in Mogadishu, and they either had no generator or it rarely worked. Bruce Bradshaw worked with the Mennonite Central Committee and taught business and economics at the National Technical Teachers Education College. His wife, Mary, volunteered at a clinic. They lived in modest expatriate homes with Somali neighbors. Our friends found ways to tolerate the frequent lack of electricity and air conditioning.

Then there were other Americans, who went to embassy-related dinner parties, sat inside watching videos, went to work, came home, and watched more videos. They lived in a foreign country but never socialized with foreigners. Some seemed oblivious to the culture of the people and really didn't want to learn about Africa.

The Buskirks

Drannon Buskirk was a consultant with Associates in Rural Development. He had a contract to survey the Juba River and determine the environmental impact of a dam that President Siad Barre wanted to build near Bardera. His wife, Carol, was active in community work. Her involvement in community projects started when she asked a Mennonite missionary, Elizabeth Nissley, for advice on where to start. Elizabeth had been working with the Somali Women's Education Department (WED) that was located in downtown Mogadishu in an old Italian Girls' school. She introduced Carol to Hawa Aden, the director of the WED. Hawa put her in touch with a sewing project. It was already operating as an income generating project for women. Young girls learned sewing and embroidery. This group also had a cooking school in another part of town.

It was a slow process to get to know the teacher of the sewing school. Carol's best contact/helper was Fatima Sharif Noor. She returned to Somalia from textile school in Manchester, UK, around the time Carol got involved at WED. Carol and Fatima developed the idea of using locally woven fabrics to make clothes.

Carol's diesel-powered back up generator, "the monster", worked most of the time. It was located right outside the dining room window and was extremely loud. She hated to use it. Rather than being a disturbance to the neighbors, the generator proved to be draw for some of the neighbors. A Somali university student next door asked if she could come over and use the light on their porch to study at night. Carol started an "English Club" when the neighbor and her friends came over to chat.

The Murdocks

The Murdocks, who were with Save the Children, also were surrounded by Somali neighbors, and had a simple, but lovely home in Mogadishu. They had neither Queen Anne furniture nor a generator. We enjoyed sitting on their porch when the power was off and appreciated the quiet. The night breeze was gentle and the flickering oil lamps casted shadows on the palm trees. The stars were so bright in the black, Somali sky that they truly glistened. The moon was more defined than in any other place. Sitting in the quiet of a Somali night, I realized that this was what I wanted. I wanted to live on a similar level with the local people – not too rough, not too comfortable. I liked the adventure of living in a new land plus being truly a part of it.

Scott

Scott Cloverdale was a young American friend who worked in a refugee camp on the Ethiopian/Somali border through the Mennonite Central Committee. He came through town on his motorcycle and would stay with us for a day or two. He must have slept on the floor, as his bed was never used.

Although he was quite reticent, we did find out that he was a construction engineer. His main interest now was in repatriating refugees back to Ethiopia. His task was to ease the refugees' dependency on free food by helping them produce their own food. Refugees were considered temporary residents in the camp and the climate was inhospitable to growing crops. Even though the experts advised him to steer clear of anything like a cooperative, he was able to organize 50 Somali farmers into a Unity Farm cooperative. Months later he could hear the "joyful shouts of farmers rose when the motor of the oily new irrigation pump started up and water flowed to their hand-dug farm plots." As Scott walked to the farm a week later, he could hear the irrigation pump thrumming and the chanting of the working farmers.

Another time Scott was talking with Ibrahim, who wanted to return to Ethiopia but still owed $15 on his treadle sewing machine. Neither he nor his family had the money. He told Scott, "I'm a God-fearing man. I won't steal it." Scott told him a story in Somali about one of the parables of Jesus: "Once there was a rich chief who had herdsman.

One owed him 50 camels...but the chief had mercy on him and forgave his debt. Then that herdsman went to a friend who owed him a packet of tea...Jesus said if God forgives our terrible sins, we should forgive each other. So, Ibrahim, it's easy to cancel your little debt on the sewing machine." The grateful refugee said, "Jesus spoke the very truth."

He had a funny story about an AID official who came to their small farming community on the Ethiopian border. The elders were sitting under the shade of a tree, eating peanuts and fruit grown on the farm, drinking honey and happily watching the harvest come in.

The AID official asked the local sheik, "What do you need?" The sheik said, "We don't need anything. We have everything that we need." The AID man replied, "I have much money and many resources." Again, the elders said, "We are alright."

The AID official insisted that they needed development. One of the Somalis finally said, "Fine, we'll take some fences and tractors". The AID man replied, "We will send some technical assistants." The sheik said, "That's good, we'll teach them how to graft fruit trees".

While Scott was here, we sat outside on the front porch, under a beautiful harvest moon, with Hassan Hussein. Scott translated some of Hassan's stories. They all had a moral such as,

- It is better to marry poor and happy than rich and miserable
- It's better to have your name spoken under a hundred shade trees than to own a hundred she-camels.

Hassan Hussein also sang for us a mournful love song in Somali about a girl. Scott was able to translate it for us. The Somalis loved to recite poetry and proverbs.

The Bradshaw's

Another Mennonite couple was Bruce and Mary Bradshaw. Mary wanted to "be in touch with the suffering people" in her area. She was teaching at the Women and Children's Hospital when she came into contact with the "Under Five Nutrition Clinic". She gave basic preventive health lessons to the mothers who had sick children in the pediatric ward.

Then she met "Medina", a baby girl who had cerebral palsy and abandoned by her mother at the Mogadishu hospital. Medina lay in her crib all day. A cleaning woman sometimes gave her a little milk. Mary was able to find a woman who would care for Medina if Mary took the baby home for one month to help improve her condition, which she did. Medina came to bless their lives. Mary saw her role as a: presence to share the Somali mothers' pain; to hold their starving babies; to listen to their concerns and to absorb their sorrow. Mary wanted to face their experiences with them.

As she cared for Medina, she learned compassion for the mothers with underweight babies. They were often pregnant again, and had little time to care for a sick child.

And that is how Mary showed her love for the Somali people.

Missionaries

Somalia is 99.9% Muslim. The Swedish Lutheran Mission began in Somalia in the 1890's, but was expelled in 1935 by Mussolini. Catholicism was introduced into Somalia in the late 19th Century. The Catholic population peaked in the 1950's at about the same time that American missionaries, the Mennonites and SIM, arrived on the shores of Somalia in the early 1950's. Throughout the years, the Mennonite mission in Somalia, Somaliland, Djibouti and Kenya had 202 missionaries that included: teachers; nurses; literacy and agricultural workers; logistics workers; administrators; horticulturists; community development workers; public health workers; animal husbandry workers; administrative assistants; dieticians; agricultural engineers; interns; Islamic Ministries; homemakers; doctors; food securities workers; hospital administrators; mission and co-mission directors; appropriate technologies workers; water resources workers; builders; physical therapy nurses; business managers; refugee workers; mechanics; secretary/bookkeepers, office assistants; country representatives; administrative assistants; agronomy workers; religious/theological educators, and justice researchers. The editor of the Missionary Messenger wrote: "In Somalia we'll face a spiritual battle intensely more difficult than any mission situation in which we've ever found ourselves." Missionaries are needed in various parts of the world, and as shown above, many vocations are put to use.

Rev. Warren Modricker, an SIM (Sudan Interior Mission) missionary, who arrived in Somalia in 1954 said, "They were lucky to get in; the

British had turned them away in 1934 saying, "No, you can't do missionary work here!" Once getting into the country the missionaries' hard work resulted in 30 to 40 Somali believers by 1963. Rev. Modricker had started by offering English classes, but also required the students to attend Bible classes at night. Religious freedom was guaranteed by the United Nations charter until June, 1963, when a new law prohibiting the propagation of any religion other than Islam came into effect. By 1973, the missionaries were ordered to vacate their property, and the Somali government nationalized all mission property and equipment.

For a Somali to convert to Christianity means losing everything, even their lives. It is also dangerous to be a missionary in Somalia. A Mennonite missionary, Merlin Groves, was murdered in 1962. He was stabbed to death by a fanatic. Three rumors existed about Merlin's murder. One story was that Merlin may have said something disparaging about Islam. More likely the mullah was agitated because copies of Mark's gospel were being distributed in Mogadishu. Another story was that the fanatic was looking for the man who preached and spoke Somali. That man was Warren Modricker. The fanatic murderer "stabbed Merlin Groves 14 to 16 times from the shoulder to the stomach, and then he was cut open right across his stomach." Mrs. Groves was stabbed also, and almost killed. She later said that "when the Somali was trying to kill her that the most wonderful love came into her heart for the Somalis! Rev. Modricker said that was the agape love. Years later Mrs. Groves returned for six months to do relief work for the Somalis. Since 1994 up to 2012, there have been 46 Somali Christian martyrs.

The Funeral

There was a young American couple with a two-year old son. They received a new contract and were celebrating at the Anglo-American Club on Lido Beach. It was a frequent stop by expatriates. The floor was made of dirt. They were remodeling it, so there were holes and debris all around. After all, this was Africa. The toddler wandered off, fell into a cistern and drowned.

On the day of the funeral, the mourners met downtown. The Murdocks drove their Land Rover with the baby casket inside. There was hardly any room for the yellow and orange flowers; their long stems were sticking out of the windows. The flowers looked so bright in that hot, Somali sun. We followed them to the cemetery....such a barren, forsaken place, right next to the ocean. There were about 12 slabs in rows, maybe more, close to each other. That's where the little boy was laid to rest. Everything looked so white: the sand, the air, the blinding sun and the crypt.

I was angry. This little boy had died in a dirty, horrible country. Here was an American child, being put in a slab on top of the ground, in a foreign, alien land.

I don't know how the parents stood it, but they were brave, and soon left Somalia. I wondered if they would, could, ever come back to see their little boy. You go to a country to try and help it, and then your son you've only had for two years, dies, before you, because of a hole in the ground? I couldn't talk to anyone about it; it was too devastating and painful. Perhaps I blamed the country, or the hole in the dirty canteen. Why didn't things work properly?

Women's International Club

One of my favorite outings was to the Women's International Club. It was held monthly at different people's homes, usually officials from the different embassies, and was a chance to meet women from different countries. We were provided food and drinks, and a guest speaker gave a talk.

I met the young wife of the German Charge d' Affairs, who was as pregnant as I was. She invited all the pregnant ladies over to her house for tea. We talked, learned some German recipes and, to my surprise, were offered beer instead of tea! That was the liveliest "tea party" I had ever attended.

Another time a German lady showed a four hour movie about a man making a trek along the Amazon River in South America, setting up opera houses. It was kind of odd to hear opera while sitting in a house in Mogadishu, but I've never forgotten the movie.

One time a Somali lady passed around incense and demonstrated how they placed the burning incense under their long dresses to give their entire body and dress the scent of the incense. The Soviet Ambassador's wife jokingly put it under her armpit, but this didn't get a big laugh.

Another reason I liked it was because there were Somali women present. I met Sofia Gaseem, whose family owned the soap factory in town. She and another Somali friend later came to my baby shower. The people were interesting and not stuffy. I also had the choice of going or not.

One day the speaker was President Siad Barre's second wife, and she shared a couple of recipes:

Recipes from Mrs. Barre's Kitchen

Somali Style Tea*

1. Boil water (quantity depends on how many you are serving)
2. While the water is boiling, grind the ginger, cardamom and cinnamon to taste.
Put these three, plus the tea, into the boiling water (the tea could be bags or loose)
3. Add the sugar and milk while the tea is boiling, but they could be added while serving.

*Somali tea is very sweet, so a large quantity of sugar can be added to the boiling water

Rice Cooked with Meat

"The Somali person does not follow a special measurement, but uses her mind. She instantly knows what quantities to use."

1. Cube meat (any type of meat can be used-fish, chicken, lamb or beef)
2. Chop onions into small pieces
3. Chop tomatoes
4. Grind cloves of garlic
5. Take a pot, add some oil. Place the pot on the heat and let some oil boil in it for few minutes.
6. Add everything into the boiling oil, cook for a while, stirring continuously.
7. When it is half done, add sufficient water and let boil for a while.

Meanwhile wash the rice.

8. When the stuff in the pot is nicely done, add rice and salt (if you want), add some butter and parmesan cheese.
Let all cook till no water is left. Then serve.

Somali Rice

1 cup of basmati rice, rinsed
2 cups chicken broth
1 medium onion, chopped
2 tsp. minced garlic
1 tsp. ground cumin
1 2-inch cinnamon sticks
3 cardamom pods
3 cloves

1. Sauté the onion and garlic in oil until it is soft.
2. Add rice and spices and continue to stir for 1 minute.
3. Add boiling chicken broth. Stir well and cover with a tight fitting lid.
4. Simmer undisturbed on low for 20 minutes.
5. Turn off heat, fluff with fork and serve."

A Somali Wedding

At one of the Women's Club meetings, Sofia Gaseem invited Carol Buskirk and me to her brother's wedding. Sofia was the ex-wife of Osman Samantar, a Somali contractor with whom Russ was familiar. Her father owned the local soap factory. Carol and I were excited to go. The event, however, turned out to be the engagement party.

When we arrived at the party, we took off our shoes, as all the Somali women did, and went upstairs into a room with a cool breeze. The women were dripping in gold and had on their best long, silky sari-type dresses. I was glad I had ordered some dresses to be made for my growing belly. I bought the material and an American friend had done the rest. It would suit me well while sitting on the carpet. A friend told us that these women were educated, accomplished and divorced at least once. Divorce is easy: the man says, "I divorce you." three times and they are divorced. They seemed to be an elite and unique group of Somali women.

The women were sitting on a huge rug. The meal began with a servant girl coming around with a kettle of water to wash our right hands. This was followed by huge trays of rice, chicken and goat meat. We ate with our right hand. I teased Carol later that she left the biggest puddle of rice on her rug! The servant girl came around after dinner, poured the water over our outstretched hands and then into a small pan. When the pan was full, she simply threw the waste water over the balcony, unconcerned about where it landed.

After dinner we were all led into another room. It had comfortable cushions scattered about, but no one sat down. Everyone started clapping and singing to the beat of a drum. One of the older ladies sang songs about how to make a good marriage. Occasionally one of the women would jump into the center of the room, put her shawl over her head and do a little dance. I began feeling faint. After all I was pregnant, so I said my good byes early. The only problem was that I couldn't find my shoes. One of the guests helped me find them, and I made a graceful exit.

The Watermelon Story

We thought we would have a quiet drive into town one day, a Friday, which was the Somali Sabbath, and there was little traffic. Being pregnant, I had a yen for watermelon, so we stopped at the first watermelon vendor. I got out to bargain while Russ and the kids waited in the truck. I asked the vendor to cut a piece, so I could see the inside and determine if it was good. He did so reluctantly, and I gave him a hundred shillings for the watermelon. A man with a red shirt standing next to the vendor interrupted and said, "No, 200 shillings!" He had piercing eyes and leaned over to me, waiting for my response. I answered, "No, one-hundred", and he became more agitated, even though he wasn't the owner of the watermelons. Russ thought the man wanted to take advantage of me and then split the extra profit with the vendor.

Soon a crowd gathered, all talking to me in Somali, Italian and English. I was tired of being cheated at the markets. I stood my ground. I asked what they would charge a Somali, and said, "My boyessa pays 60 shillings, and I'm offering one hundred." I had bargained, when I lived in Mexico and assumed this was the same way vendors operated worldwide. The main problem as an outsider was not having a good idea of what the starting price should be. Something that I thought was cheap at 100 shillings; a Somali would pay only 50 shillings.

The man in the red shirt took the watermelon and started talking to Russ, who bargained him down to 150 shillings. Meanwhile some kids talking to me said, "You could get a better deal down the street." I moved through the maze of people back to the truck, called Russ and we left on a sour note. These were just the daily hassles, but it seemed to needle me particularly that day.

We continued on our drive to the city center around the Croce del Sud Hotel, and came upon some street urchins who asked for "baksheesh" (money). They ignored our mayas (no), and started running with the truck, when Laura saw one of the boys take the rubber cap off the door lock before darting away. We turned the truck around, and this time we were running after the kids. Who did we think we were? I don't know. We thought we saw one of the boys hand something to a man standing on the street, before they disappeared into an alley. We confronted the man, but he denied knowing what we were talking about.

I didn't know if we were frustrated by: people trying to rip us off; fighting street kids; driving in a town with no stoplights and kamikaze drivers; one-hundred degree heat; fighting the donkeys and goats in the streets, or general malaise. I don't think I was in the mood for an adventure. We decided to drive around some more, and if we saw the boys, we would squirt them with a water bottle we had in the truck.

We did find the boys. Just as Russ was about to lift the water bottle and take aim, one of the boys produced a can of water and poured it.......not on us, but over the head of the boy whom we thought was the major culprit! This broke the spell, and everyone laughed. The boys thought it was great fun, and we felt good again. With our spirits lifted, we drove back to the watermelon man. This time there was no man with a red shirt and no crowd, so we easily bought the watermelon for 100 shillings.

On the way home we stopped at the Makka Hotel's coffee shop and ordered cake, watermelon juice and cappuccino. When we left, I was carrying a piece of cake that Katie hadn't finished. Before climbing into the car I took a bite of the cake. It was so dry and stale it wasn't worth saving, so I threw it on the ground. From out of nowhere came a pack of street urchins who fought over the discarded cake, like sharks in a feeding frenzy. (Years later I would pay more attention to the street urchins). When the hotel doorman in a bright red jacket tried to lift Katie into the truck, he accidentally bumped her head. Katie turned around and yelled "stop it". That ended our "quiet" drive on the Somali Sabbath.

The Chicken Story

Russ flippantly said to both Hassan's that we should try to raise chickens, so we could have eggs. The next day Hassan Hussein brought a rooster to the door, and we were faced with the decision of whether to eat the rooster or raise chickens. We decided to get a couple of hens and see what happened.

We made a big, wooden box into a cage for the chickens to roost. They were cheap, but they didn't lay many eggs. They also made a big mess around the yard and on the porch.

We heard chickens also brought lice, which Katie ended up getting. The lice didn't completely go away until we went to London. We also didn't like the idea that baboons started appearing on our wall, and we thought they were looking for the chickens.

We decided to get rid of the chickens. We gave one chicken to Sucre, one to Hassan Ali and one to Hassan Hussein. There was one chicken left.

"Let us give it to Isman," Sucre suggested. Isman was the neighbor's watchman. He had two wives, so I was reluctant to give him the extra chicken.

"No," I said shaking my head, "he has two wives."

"No, Sister, he has many children.", and the chicken went to Isman.

I thought it was settled, when a couple nights later Hassan Hussein told me, "Sister Pat, Isman has taken all the chickens, and Sucre is going to sell the big box!" Shucre had told me that she wanted the box for a cupboard.

Isman, the neighbor's watchman, said, "We all agreed that I should keep the chickens at my place, and that Sucre was not going to sell the box."

The next day I talked to Sucre, and she went into a tirade about Hassan. "He is stupid!" she shouted, "stupid, and no good! He is always asking you for something!"

She was partly right about him asking for things. Hassan Hussein was Russ' favorite. He had learned how to ride a bike, and he played with the kids all of the time. Later I spoke with Hassan.

"Hassan," I said gently, "Shucre is very upset. She is mad that you came to us and told us that she was going to sell the box." Hassan responded by saying, "Sucre is good and always cleans my clothes." After telling this to Sucre, she softened and said, "Did he really say I was good?"

I never envisioned that giving the chickens away would be so complicated, or that a tough, wiry Somali watchman would have such grace in response to a criticism.

Cross-Cultural Experiences

Russ

During one of our trips outside of the city, we passed through the town of Wanle Weyn. We noticed a group of women gathered around herdsman pouring milk from a homemade Hahn, a large jug, into the women's dheel, or smaller jugs. This looked like a good place to strike a bargain on one of those jugs that we admired so much, because they were handmade and functional.

I watched as Pat walked up the women and, after quite a bit of talking and hand motioning, came back to the car with a nice dheel. The dheel was a good deal at 300 shillings. The women were smiling and laughing, so we assumed they felt it was a good deal too. However, when Pat got into the car and we started to drive off, they began yelling and ran up to the car. They wanted the jug back! The women thought we wanted to buy the milk and were foolish enough to pay 300 shillings for the milk.

After a bit of haggling and some assistance from an onlooker who spoke a little English, we ended up with a different jug. The women couldn't understand why we were trying to give them back the milk that was in the jug. In fact, after pouring the milk into an empty baby formula can, one woman insisted that we take the can of milk with the jug. She couldn't believe that we wanted a jug and no milk

I had a similar cross-cultural experience one day while walking through the bush with our neighbor, Tommy Allen, hunting for warthogs with a bow and arrow. The Allen's were one of the three families with whom we shared the compound. They all worked for the embassy in fairly sensitive positions and they had kids. It was good for us to have neighbors with whom to share family experiences. Tommy was fond of Africa. His house was filled with African books, rugs, jugs, headrests and spears. He enjoyed buying jugs and headrests and talking about clans as much as I did. His wife was a superb cook, and the first time Pat saw a Martha Stewart cookbook was in her home. This was Pat's introduction to Martha Stewart - in Mogadishu, of all places on earth.

On this particular day, we came upon a Somali woman with her children and a few goats. I happened to be drinking a can of Coke that I carried with me, and I handed it to the mother. She took a sip and passed the can to a daughter, who then took a sip and passed the can to a young boy. He took a small sip, made a face and spat out the Coke. I then realized that this boy had probably never drunk anything other than water and warm milk. This cola was as foreign to him as warm camel milk would be to my children

The Shabelli River

Russ

The Shabelli River flows out of Ethiopia and courses south toward Mogadishu. Before reaching Mogadishu and the Indian Ocean, it veers southwest and disintegrates into a marshy expanse between Jilib and Barawe. The waters of the Shabelli never reach the Indian Ocean, and they fall short of meeting the Juba. The area along the Shabelli River is, of course, a prime agricultural area. History along the Shabelli is the history of southern Somalia.

The coastal cities of Somalia established early trade links with the Arabian Gulf and Persia. Agricultural commodities from the Shabelli valley enabled Mogadishu to maintain its dominant role in such trade. Just as the coast drew trade from distant continents, the Shabelli River Valley drew migrating people groups from other parts of the Horn of Africa. Some archeologists and linguistics experts claim that the ancestors of today's Somali-speakers inhabited the riverine regions of the south before occupying the arid, northern regions of Somalia.

The early Bantu-speaking settlers in the Lower Shabelli Region had frequent contact with nomadic herdsmen who came from various parts of the Horn to seek refuge and green pastures along the river valley. Many of the nomads stayed and mixed farming with livestock herding. Coastal people, many of Arab descent, came to the valley for trade, and some set up trading posts. This intermingling of people from various nomadic clans, the settled farmers and the coastal traders evolved into a group of Somali-speaking people with a shared identity. This group is primarily represented by the Rahanwein clan.

Many of our outings took place along the Shabelli River. Laura's Girl Scout troop from the American School had a campout along the river near Balad. I joined the campers and a couple of other parents, including our friends, Drannon and Carol Buskirk, who were leading the troop.

Laura and I thought we were pretty smart, having brought a two-man pup tent from the States. After arriving at the campsite, everyone got busy unloading and setting up tents. We finished putting up our tent and stepped back to look at it, but it seemed somehow out of place. The Buskirk's external-frame, high-tech, nylon, ten-person domed tent dwarfed our little pup tent. A French couple had a classic, canvas tent with veranda, cots and folding chairs. Their tent was from the movie set of Out of Africa, and ours was from a Marine Corps boot camp. Laura and I were "out tented", but it wasn't too embarrassing.

We did gain respect from a local "hunter-gatherer" with our modern bow. This old man with a primitive bow and poisoned arrows was hired to stand guard on the campsite overnight. His bow didn't have much pull-weight. When the old man shot an arrow, he lunged forward and threw the arrow as much as he shot it. Animals that were wounded by an arrow shot in such a manner would be tracked for days, until they died from the trace of powerful poison that got into their system. In the morning we got out our archery set, and the girls practiced shooting arrows. The old man was impressed with the trajectory of the arrows shot by our "dime store" archery set. He still preferred his old tree limb to our new fangled fiberglass bow that we brought to shoot Coke cans along the bank of the Shabelli River.

From Balad, the Shabelli River winds north of Mogadishu through the town of Afgoye. Afgoye was the center for the powerful Geledi clan who ruled the Lower Shabelli in the 18th century. They succeeded the iron-fisted dominance of the Ajuran Confederation who controlled southern Somalia from the 15th to the 18th Century. The Ajuran are an enigma. Some scholars say that they are from the lineage of Dir. Many Somalis say that they did not originate from any of the Somali patriarchs, so there is no agreement about their clan origins. Since their downfall in the 18th Century, the Ajuran have been a clan without a home and are simply scattered throughout the Horn of Africa.

Afgoye was the home of the "Ishtun" stick fights. This annual spectacle consisted of two groups of men on each side of a field. At the signal they charged to the center of the field and hit each other with sticks under the searing sun. There were seldom any fatalities, but the legend stated that the more blood that was spilled, the better would be the coming harvest. The fights were delayed the time we attended, although I don't think there was a formal schedule. We mostly ate sugar cane straight from the field while the hot sun beat down on us sitting in the stands. We ended up being evicted from the viewing stands by the Darod cops. They really enjoyed kicking us expats off the stands.

Marka was an old, Italian port town south of Mogadishu. The Barracuda Restaurant was on a hill at the edge of town and was a favorite place for expatriates to visit. We arrived in the middle of the afternoon, having taken the inland route from Afgoi to Shalambod through farming areas that looked like eastern North Carolina. The roads were mostly crumbled tarmac. The restaurant didn't seem to be ready for business at the strange time of our arrival, but they served pasta and grilled fish that would have been good even if we weren't starving.

The beaches at Marka, like everywhere else in Somalia, were wide, isolated expanses of sand. The town of Marka consisted of weather-worn stone buildings and fortifications. Nothing appeared to be newer than 14th century construction.

The day after we returned to Mogadishu from our journey on the bumpy road to Marka, a wheel bearing broke on our old Peugeot. This was when I learned how ingenious mechanics were in the Third World at keeping a car on the road. Our Peugeot was refitted with a Chevy wheel bearing from the American Embassy motor pool, and the car was back on the road in two days.

TRIP TO LONDON

November, 1986

Russ

Pat was approaching full term in her pregnancy, so we arranged a trip to London to have the baby. The night airplane ride was a tough squeeze for a nine-month pregnant woman. Pat drifted on and off in sleep and her ankles were swelling up. Laura and I were looking forward to having a Big Mac, and Pat was going to get a haircut and buy lotions and creams.

The lifestyle in Europe seemed more humane than the pace of life in the U.S. People walked to neighborhood stores to do their shopping, and talked to each other on the street. We rented a flat in Wimbledon and bought meat from the butcher shop, fish from the fishmonger and fresh fruit and vegetables from a street corner stand. Unlike the tedium of driving to a supermarket for a week's supply of groceries, it was a pleasure to walk to the shops and choose fresh ingredients for the day's meals.

The cost of living in London was very high, but the "pub grub" was a good deal. Simple, hardy food such as generous portions of cottage pie and steak and kidney pie, stuffed with plenty of meat, was fairly cheap. I also acquired a taste for bitters. Drawn from a tap and served warm, my first sip tasted like dish water. I soon appreciated its crisp, unique taste which had more snap than lager.

Nothing beats the thrill of seeing a great city for the first time. On our first subway ride into London from Wimbledon, we picked a stop that looked from the map to be in a central area with some points of interest nearby. The anticipation built as we climbed to street level not knowing what sights were in store for us. As we reached the last step and looked up, Big Ben was towering over us. It was an allegorical Welcome to London that couldn't have been better if Prime Minister Maggie Thatcher had met us on the top step.

Katie, at age 3, didn't do too well on our subsequent subway rides. We were packed into a car with hundreds of other passengers getting on and off at each stop. We were pushed further into the corner each time the train stopped. Halfway to our destination Katie yelled "I have to go to the bathroom!" This brought giggles from some of the other passengers. We didn't think it was funny, because we knew Katie would get hysterical if she didn't get to a bathroom soon. While Pat was in the Humana Hospital in St. John's Wood, Laura, Katie and I made the trip almost daily from Wimbledon by the train. The most direct route required three transfers, which was difficult for a three year-old, so we started taking a longer route that required only two transfers.

The girls and I spent quite a bit of time in the parks. We found a little playground tucked away in Regents Park where pre-school and kindergarten teachers brought their classes. We enjoyed the ambiance of Hyde Park with the ducks gliding on the pond, the squirrels jumping from tree limb to tree limb and, of course, the nannies with big, black baby buggies. I had only seen such carriages with their large spoke wheels in period movies and antique shops. This was a stark contrast to the American fold-up, umbrella strollers which are easy and convenient for the parents to handle. The baby buggies are much more practical for walks in the park when the weather may be drizzly. This is probably why they remain so much in use in London.

Great and Little Wolford

My family moved to Columbus, Ohio, from the small villages and farming area of Roscoe, Ohio. According to the Library of Congress, the Wolford family originated from the towns of Great Wolford and Little Wolford in England. The Wolfords were between Oxford and Stratford-upon-Avon, near the Cotswold's. This was a picturesque land of rolling hills, nestled villages and eccentricity. The sheep grazed in green, rolling pastures bordered by rows of mixed hardwood trees, trimmed hedges and chest-high stone walls. The small towns were a composite of family-run shops and businesses with crests and coats of arms prominently displayed. The physical structures were preserved and maintained to do justice to the period in which they were built.

Little Wolford consisted of a few stately, brick homes sitting in an open lowlands area. The road through Little Wolford curved over the ford and up a hill to Great Wolford which consisted of a mix of cottages and larger houses with walled gardens and trimmed hedges, a church with a cemetery, a post office and a pub. We talked to a lady placing flowers on the altar at the church - Eleanor Rigby? She stated that no Wolfords had ever appeared on the church rolls and none were buried in the cemetery. She reckoned that the name was used by people from one of the Wolfords when they moved to America. She said, "Many people changed their name on the voyage because they were running away from something. It was easy for John, from Wolford, to live with the name of John Wolford."

We looked at the tombstones, and many of the names were Fletcher. Maybe our family name was really Fletcher. The cemetery overlooked a green valley broken occasionally by rows of hedges and the road leading through Little Wolford. We stopped at the local pub and had the best steak and kidney pie of the trip. It had dark walls, timber beams and a low ceiling. The proprietor told us about a well known ghost who visits the pub and sits at the end of the bar. The pub wasn't unique, but it was old. It was like the setting of an old horror movie in the scene where the men of the village are huddled on a rainy night around a glimmering fire as a stranger comes in asking for directions through the moor.

Arrival of Ryan Andrew Wolford

Pat

I loved going to the see my doctor on Harley Street, a famous street for doctors. In London things seemed so proper. I was amused at how the British correctly stood in lines or queues, as opposed to Americans who stood in clusters. Outside of the doctor's office was a high, black iron fence. The door to the office was huge and the waiting room was expansive. There was a grand fireplace. A friend of ours from Raleigh was living in London for a year and had recommended this doctor and found the little flat in Wimbledon where we stayed for a month.

After having two children, I decided to go the "painless" way of birth with a shot in my back. This, of course, was not totally painless. We were scheduled for noon, and Ryan Andrew was born on November 27, 1986. The first few minutes when the doctor was patting him on the butt and waiting for his first breath seemed like an eternity. Ryan's birth certificate was issued in Westminster and signed by the same lady who signed Prince William's birth certificate.

The Humana Hospital was very pleasant. My roommate in the maternity ward was a French woman. She was speaking in French a lot, but what I would gather was that she was having trouble suckling her baby. I silently prayed and finally her milk let down!

Since Ryan was born on Thanksgiving, I asked if they had any turkey dinners. They checked with the chef, who was American, and I had my turkey dinner in the hospital the day after Thanksgiving. It tasted so good!

Russ

We spent another week in London, and then Ryan was ready for his first airplane ride.

When we changed planes in Nairobi, an expediter was waiting to help people make their connections. He looked at our tickets then disappeared down a stairway. When he came back, he said that we owed $175 for excess baggage through to Mogadishu. We had paid a lesser amount in London which I thought covered excess baggage all of the way to Mogadishu. Apparently it hadn't. I offered to write a check to the airline, but our expediter said that a check was not acceptable – only cash. Something was fishy, but we had to play along. I pointed out that we were on the last leg of our journey and only had $25. He insisted that this would not be sufficient, and I insisted that he go back downstairs and explain the situation to whomever was in charge.

It is sometimes helpful in such situations to bring an imaginary third person into the picture. Our friend soon returned and said he could get our bags onto the plane for $30. We scraped together the money, and we and our bags were eventually on our way. We boarded the plane which was filled to capacity with Somalis and the bags that they picked up in Nairobi.

Boarding a Somali Airways flight was like a reverse fire drill. Seats were not assigned, so we had to hustle to get five seats together. It then occurred to me that if all of these people slipped $175 worth of excess baggage onto the plane by paying $30 "baksheesh" then this plane isn't getting off the ground. The plane made it off the ground, but back in Mogadishu my career was going to go down in flames. Furthermore, the family wasn't too excited about returning to Somalia.

BACK IN MOGADISHU

Pat

The wind had really picked up since our return. It swirled the dust around into little funnels along the road. Dust particles settled in our hair and grit got into our teeth.

Most of my time was spent in the house, around the compound or with Americans. I didn't want to be back. I didn't want to look out the window and see Africa. I just wanted to stay in our house and not look at Africa. Finally, a Somali friend invited me to a tea party. It was enjoyable and it helped me to get back into my Mogadishu routine.

I took my first drive downtown and almost got into an accident. I forgot you have to pay attention and not daydream like on Western freeways. I stopped at a new store, but they didn't have anything different. I then walked to a shop on the corner where they had fresh ground coffee. I noticed the bright lights in the store, because most shops are dark inside, and the Egyptian sounding music playing.

I panicked outside of the store, because the car wouldn't start. A man with a deformed arm kept asking for baksheesh, in a soft voice over and over. The vegetable man kept asking if I wanted tomatoes. The fruit man kept asking if I wanted bananas, and a lady sitting on the curb kept saying "missus, missus, missus"! I said, "No, no, no, I don't want anything. No baksheesh". I rolled down all of the windows, because it was getting very hot, and the beggar leaned over expecting a hand-out. I smiled and said "no". He was leaning on the car, and I was looking around to see if anyone was around to help.

A stocky, Italian man was arguing over the price of vegetables, and another Italian and his wife had just gone into the store. The beggar suddenly started to push the car. I nodded my head to say it wouldn't work, and then the car started. I smiled. He smiled and moved away. I said "Suq, suq (wait)!" and handed him a dollar bill, a sizable amount of baksheesh. I had to wipe egg off my face, but it was then that I started noticing the poverty.

At the end of February, 1987, the hot, desert winds have abruptly subsided. Instead of whistling wind and thick dust, we had oppressive heat and headaches to match. It was so hot that the swimming pool water in K-7 in the American compound felt like a bath.

I seem to be attending a lot of baby showers these days. The time had come for some of the pregnant women to give birth.

The Tonga Friend

Local sports were a big thing with us at this time. Laura and our young lady friend, Teuu, who was from Tonga in the Polynesian Islands, had started soccer matches with the Somali boys of our neighborhood outside of our gate in the alley. We started getting an older crowd who were very earnest. Many of the Somalis played barefoot and seemed very good. The Somali boys would wait outside of our gate each evening. If Laura and Teuu were not playing, they would use our soccer ball.

Teuu was in her twenties and great fun to have around. She was young, almost thirty years younger than George, her crusty English husband, who was with her all the time (he was the only male at my baby shower). He had lived in Africa most of his life. She was full of life and laughter. She and George lived a Spartan life in a little house, with handmade art made of grass from Tonga on the walls. She gave a woodcut of zebras made of parchment paper to Laura. We had ice cream sodas one evening at our house that George drank with relish. He said that he had almost forgotten that they had existed.

We went to their house one night for a cookout. It was held on the roof. Teuu used coconut shells for fuel. We provided one of the barbecue grills, and the coconut shells burned so hot that it melted the paint off the grill. It was a good cookout with fish, beef and chicken, as well as some new vegetable dishes.

Bringing up Baby

I learned what other mothers meant when they said, "I have to watch him every minute". Ryan chewed on lamp cords and knocked over tables. He rolled around a lot and smiled at anyone who looked at him. He often went to sleep by himself. He would take some sort of material to cover his face, stick his thumb in his mouth and cover his eyes with his arm. Many times Russ would hold him on his shoulder, walking gently around the Queen Anne dining room table, until Ryan's head finally fell on his shoulder, asleep.

For Ryan's baptism I had my dress and Ryan's outfit made out of the same cloth. We decided to have him baptized by an American Universalist preacher, against our better judgment. She started her benediction and was talking about the moon, the sky, the earth and the stars. Russ interrupted her and said we were baptizing him in the name of Jesus. Then she added "And Jesus! Oh yes, and the Father, Son and Holy Ghost!"

Katie was "using her words" more and screaming less. She either loved or hated every minute, and seemed revved up to ninety miles an hour inside her little body. For her two year old birthday party, three of her little friends came over (all boys). We had a small, plastic pool for them to splash in on the porch. The blustery winds blew the birthday decorations every which way. She enjoyed the party!

Laura was still struggling to accept living in Somalia. We continued to go to the swimming pools, and walked to nearby cafes or hotels for breakfast on the outside verandas. At night we could go to the outdoor movies on the American compound. Laura wasn't scared of anything in Somalia, except the baboons that occasionally appeared on our wall, but they were easily chased away. Laura visited other people's houses in the compound, where American videos were the great distraction. Meanwhile, I tried to help Laura and Katie memorize Bible verses.

Conflicts Everywhere

Pat and Russ

Russ' job was going well and he enjoyed the occasional intrigue of mission politics. A friend of the USAID Director didn't get a big contract. This caused much discussion among the USAID people and local Somalis. From Russ' perspective, the result was good for USAID because it showed that the contracting procedures were honest.

Sofia Gaseem, the Somali lady who invited me to a wedding shower and who attended my baby shower, was also the ex-wife of Osman Samantar, the director's friend who lost the contract. He had become Russ' major antagonist. Sofia and her family didn't have good things to say about Samantar. The more people you knew, the more intriguing Mogadishu became. A big rift was forming with Samantar, the director and his sycophants on one side and Russ, the Gaseems and the Isaaqs (who won the contract) on the other. It was like a battle, one side for Samantar and the Director and the other side for an honest business man.

Mogadishu was a hardship post for all foreigners: USAID and UN employees; World Bank; European donors; missionaries and development people. That's why it was a two year stint, instead of four. People tried to make the best of the situation. There was an undercurrent of craziness in Somalia and among people working there. We heard that one power outage was due to the fact that the Somalis were using the fresh water supply necessary for power generation to wash their cars.

Another example was that the expatriate technicians were often called to fix the solar panels at a Somali government ministry. It was a hard, four hour drive by the European technicians to simply: clean the dust off the panels!

There were various conflicts in the American community. Teachers in the school lost patience with each other. Some USAID employees stabbed each other in the back whenever they had a chance. Many careers were ruined in Mogadishu. One time we counted the number of people fired, and the number of affairs and divorces.

One always had to be on their guard against bugs, diseases, shopping in the markets, bartering for food, the heat and dust, driving kamikaze with no traffic lights working, what to fix for three meals a day, goats eating the garbage along the streets, people yelling and not knowing what they were saying, on top of being exhausted all the time.

One time I did go crazy. I was crying in the bedroom, and called Russ to come home early from work. My mind was out of control and I was crying uncontrollably. It wasn't that I missed America so much, as I was overwhelmed by Mogadishu.

Even before we left London, I was determined to let Shucre go. I suppose the last straw was when I told Shucre we needed butter, and she told me to get it myself. What made it easier was that the people who had stayed at our place while we were in London had some things missing. I don't know if Shucre took anything or not, but I did not want to share the house with her. My heart was hardened and I refused to see her at all.

Russ wasn't in agreement with me, but he told her we didn't need her anymore. She was shocked, and told Russ that I had too much to worry about with the new baby. Russ told her we didn't need her help. Laura was present during all this, and got upset.

I never saw Shucre again, although she came almost daily for a week outside our compound wall. The last time she came, she had a baby with her. Laura went out and gave her a ten pound note from England out of her own money. Shucre had named her baby, Laura.

I've thought about Shucre and her baby every since, and whether during the passing years they survived the war and chaos in Somalia. If I had to do it over again......

FALL OF THE SOMALIST

Russ

Osman Samantar was an engaging fellow, sociable, personable and a good conversationalist. He was a typical USAID pariah who gained the trust and admiration of the mission director's wife. He had several USAID contracts including a major contract for field support to the many consultants and contract personnel who worked for the mission. Any housing, supplies, security and support for contract personnel was handled under this field support contract. His main agenda was to talk the AID Director into giving him sole source contracts which meant he wouldn't have to compete. It would be a gift.

One time Samantar visited our house in the evening, unannounced, ostensibly to introduce us to his new wife. He was surprised to see a Somali Bible written in the Somali language. It had been given to us by a retired missionary, Rev. Modricker. We also had the Koran in English on our bookshelf. This opened a discussion about religion. Proselytizing was illegal in Somalia, but discussions such as these were appropriate. As he was leaving, he asked to borrow the Somali Bible and the Koran so he could "compare" them. Pat had reservations because she thought he really wasn't that interested in it, and suspicious because he came to our house unannounced. Pat also had formed a friendship with his ex-wife, Sofia. In the end, we gave both the Bible and Koran to him. The field support contract was nearing expiration, and a new contract was to be open to competition. Since I was the Contracting Officer, it was my responsibility to handle the procurement.

Doing business in Somalia was different that doing business in America. Somali businessmen didn't specialize. They went wherever there was money was to be made, and honestly thought that they could do any job. Construction companies bid for accounting work. Accounting firms bid on agricultural feasibility studies, and the ubiquitous import-export outfits, with some credibility, competed for any type of work.

Of the sixty companies that submitted some sort of proposal for the contract, twenty were serious and eight presented good proposals. This was high visibility procurement, and created much interest in the Somali business community. The USAID mission's credibility was on the line, and the contracting procedures had to be flawless. As a result of an exhaustive evaluation, a new contractor was selected for the field support contract.

The company that won the contract was run by a couple of Isaaqs named Aden Omar Awaleh and Aden Nur Awaleh. Their financial backing was from a wealthy uncle in England who was "persona non grata" with the Somali government. The rumor was that he had a falling out with Siad Barre, the President of Somalia, and couldn't return to Somalia. His relatives, however, continued to care for and expand his business interests in Mogadishu. The two Adens were competent, and they knew how to work with Western aid agencies as well as how to work in Somalia.

After losing the contract, Samantar had one of his friends in the Ministry of Labor send a letter to the mission stating that the new contractor was not permitted to do such business in Somalia. Aden Nur contacted one of his clansmen in the Ministry of Labor, who produced a document stating that they were indeed registered to do such business.

The USAID Director initially seemed resigned to the fact that Samantar lost the contract. His wife, however, didn't take the news so well. I heard that she even grumbled about it at parties. The director's attitude soon changed, and I received several inflammatory memos from him complaining about the result of the procurement. The die was cast, however. The new contractor was selected using proper contracting procedures, and there was no turning back.

The director got in the last word on my next performance evaluation. He said I had a bad work ethic and sat in the café too long. The controller was also quoted as saying I had a laid back "California" attitude. Among these types of negative comments, the director stated that I had been distributing Bibles to Somalis. I asked him where he got that idea, and he said, "Osman Samantar." Samantar lost a contract, but I lost a job.

Since I didn't have tenure in the Foreign Service, the bad evaluation resulted in the loss of my appointment. I made an attempt to nullify the evaluation and retain my job by filing an appeal. The Appeals Board did agree that the evaluation was prejudicial and unfounded, and I even received a small, cash settlement for certain damages. There was a hitch, however, that since I had a limited rather than tenured appointment, the board did not have the authority to reinstate my job.

My firing was a scandal in Mogadishu. The Somalis were skeptical of the entire contracting process and thought that it was a charade. Most thought that surely Samantar would get the contract, since he was a friend of the director. Some thought the son-in-law of the Somali ambassador to the U.S. would have an inside line. They were surprised, and the USAID mission gained much respect when an honest, competitive businessman got the contract.

Pat

The kids and I had taken a brief vacation back to the U.S. while I got my eyes checked, while Russ stayed in Somalia. Taking a Swiss jumbo jet was new and exciting. I was fully prepared for the long trip home, with blankies, treats, toys, backpacks and books. I balanced Ryan on my knee while feeding him baby food, and attempted to simultaneously keep an eye on Katie and Laura. It seemed indomitable through the long flight, but I got it done. I didn't look up to see if people were watching, and tried to clean up the messes, feed the baby and soothe the children.

The Swiss stewardesses were very kind and were the only ones who asked if I needed help throughout the entire journey. It brought tears to my eyes, but I looked down, as I did indeed need help, and wondered how I would make it through the next flight to the U.S. Their smiles and concern built me up for the next leg, and I wound my way through a new airport with my three little ones in tow. If I had had Russ with me, I probably wouldn't have noticed the helpful stewardesses and just taken them for granted. How often do we not really "see" people and ignore them? How many times have I dropped the ball and didn't take the time to encourage others or say a friendly word. Jesus spoke to others in His path; can I do the same? In all the chaos, the girls' favorite blankies went missing. But we had the U.S. to look forward to.

We visited my brother and his family in Chicago. It was wonderful to be back, and we made friends with their neighbors. We enjoyed a lovely few weeks swimming on Lake Michigan, eating ice cream cones and riding bikes.

I was sitting on the grass watching the kids play and talking with a neighbor. She was asking me if I would be interested in buying a set of Encyclopedias. I seriously considered it because it would be helpful for the kids. The $700 seemed daunting, but I thought we could do it. I was ready to sign up. Then the call came from Russ in Somalia.

"Pat, I've been fired." he said abruptly, even before I had a chance to say hello.

The shock was evident in his voice. "I'll be coming back in a few weeks, so you have to stay where you are," he continued. I was struck-it was like having something put in your mouth that is too big, and it lands in your stomach like a table, and you don't know how to get it out.

"What do you mean?" I asked, struggling to make sense of the unexpected news.

"I don't know. I got a bad evaluation. The director made negative comments throughout the entire thing. He said I've been distributing Bibles to Somalis!"

"What? Why would he say that?" I asked, anger building up inside me. I immediately thought back to the evening when Samantar visited our house and asked for the Bible.

"I asked him." Russ continued, "I asked him where he got that idea, and he said 'Osman Samantar'." Of course.

"What are you doing to do?" I asked, weakly, the implications of not being able to return to Somalia began settling into my heart.

"I'm going to appeal it, of course," he said, "but it will take time."

"Do you think the Board will rule in your favor?" I asked. Russ said, "I think they will." I could sense the urgency in his voice.

"Well, you are the first Contract Officer in that post. You were trying to set up the proper procedures. If you had tenure, maybe they wouldn't have been able to do this." It was true, but I imagined it was little consolation to him now.

"We'll talk about it later," he said. "I need to take care of some things before I leave."

"Okay," I said.

I stood in the kitchen with the receiver still in my hand. What would I tell my brother and sister-in-law with whom we were staying? My father had been so proud of Russ for making it in the Foreign Service. But he hadn't made it after all.

My life in Somalia was over. I didn't want to go back to Ohio. I didn't think of the money. I suppose I thought that this would be Russ' life work, and we could live overseas. I thought of him alone in Mogadishu and wondered how he was doing, if anyone visited him, and what our neighbors thought. I didn't realize then how much Somalia and Somalis were in our blood and that we would find 20,000 Somalis in our hometown years later.

Out of Africa

Russ

As the equatorial sun peaked over the dusty streets and whitewashed buildings of Mogadishu, I prepared to leave Somalia. I thought I would have my whole career with USAID. I wanted to establish a contracting office and make their contracts work right, which I did. Now, a sense of urgency overwhelmed me. I had to get it settled. I anticipated a resolution by the board in my favor, but that would take time. I wasn't thinking about how I might miss Somalia. I only thought that I should not have come here in the first place.

Somalia, then became, a life's vocation, if it is possible for a country to become a life's vocation. Isn't it ironic that a place and a people that you keep having conflict with is your life's vocation? Some people's life vocation is to do what they want to do. I wanted to be a cowboy when I was a kid, not a Somalist.

There were key people that I remember relating to at the end. Hassan Ali and Hassan Hussein, our guards, were disappointed at our leaving. Hawa's sons joined me on the ride to the airport. At the airport, I specifically remembered several of the Isaaqs helping me get through the VIP departure lounge. If it weren't for them, I would have just been any ordinary passenger getting on the plane, but they saw to it that I had a smooth departure at the airport.

There were definitely good guys and bad guys involved in our assignment in Somalia and subsequent departure. I often forget about the bad guys, but always hope to see the good guys sometime again.

Several years later in the Northern Frontier District of Kenya, I even asked some Dagodi if they knew Hassan Hussein Handule. He was not in their immediate sub clan, but they said they would try to find him for me. Neither they, nor any of the Dagodi that I saw in Nairobi later, were able to help me find him. I'm sure that he made it out of Somalia since his clan's territory was on the border of Ethiopia and Kenya. Hassan Ali, however, was an Abgal from Mogadishu, and there's a good chance he got caught up in heavy fighting in the civil war.

I boarded a Somali Airways 707 and headed west to a new place and a new adventure. Somalia remained in our hearts like the good parts of a love affair that you recall years later. We did not forget Mogadishu; it remained a part of us. We would return to Somalia, but it wouldn't be the same.

Once in Mogadishu I thought, "Wouldn't it be neat to live on a farm in southern Delaware County and go hunting everyday". Seriously, I thought that. Believe it or not, one result of getting kicked out of the Foreign Service was that I ended up on a farm in southern Delaware County, Ohio thanks to an old friend, Lowell Shoaf. I didn't get my government job back. I had no career, but I lived in a farm house and went hunting any time I wanted. One day while walking in the field, I got an epiphany: "I will find a Christian organization to work with and be a missionary." I had never thought of such a thing before, but it seemed like a good idea. The light went on. Pat was secretly happy, because she had always had a desire to be a missionary. We started researching information on Christian organizations working overseas.

Pat

Russ filed a grievance, but he wasn't tenured and couldn't get his job back. He did get a small financial settlement. The children were enrolled in the country schools, and Laura joined a soccer team. Russ sold Buicks. His steadfastness helped give us a foundation of security. When he had his epiphany in Delaware County, Ohio, of working for a Christian organization, we researched different Christian organizations that were working overseas. It seemed like many were volunteer positions.

We received a pamphlet in the mail from Habitat for Humanity, but I threw it in the trash. It looked like a volunteer organization, and we needed some sort of pay check. We received the same pamphlet a month later, and this time we took a closer look. It was about building houses for poor people in different countries. Volunteers did get a "stipend". I didn't know anything about building houses, but Russ did. He had worked his way through college as a carpenter. We headed south to Americus, Georgia!

Americus, the headquarters for Habitat for Humanity, was about an hour south of Atlanta. To the east of Americus were peach orchards. The area around Americus was mostly pecan trees. Just west of Americus was the Plains, Georgia and the heart of peanut country. We drove to Jimmy Carter's church, and shook hands with him. He was a big advocate for Habitat for Humanity.

The more we learned about Habitat, the more we liked it. It was an opportunity to live with the locals in another country and to actually provide direct help to individuals. We liked the other Habitat trainees and enjoyed socializing with them. They were younger than we were, and wore flip flops. This was O.K., even though I always wore pants and work boots. I claimed there were two types of development men: those in flip flops and those in boots, and the most effective ones were those in boots.

It was a pleasant time: we had hope for the future and were training for our next assignment. This was even a good summer for the kids. They enjoyed the day care and being around the different people in a beautiful southern summer. One day we drove out into the countryside and visited a communal type farm, Koinanea. We had lunch, with heaping portions of home-grown food. In the sticky hot, Georgia, summer sun, we picked blueberries.

The major question and concern for all Habitat volunteers was where they would be assigned. We actually heard that we were considered for Peru, but the situation changed, and we were assigned to Papua New Guinea. Pat burst into tears, because she didn't want to go to Papua New Guinea. Our last couple of weeks in Americus was spent studying Pidgin.

It sounded like butchered English, but to Papua New Guineans, it is a legitimate way to communicate between tribes.

Our travel arrangements were different than those on our trip to Somalia. This time we had no excess baggage and no air shipment, just two bags for each person. We travelled light and found that it was good to be agile and flexible.

PART II
PORT MORESBY, PAPUA NEW GUINEA
1990-1992

Our Assignment

Pat

"Is there any group you could not work with?" the tall and thin interviewer at Habitat for Humanity asked. I immediately replied, "Yes, Pentecostals". Three months later we arrived in a taxi right in the middle of a Pentecostal church compound, ready to work with Habit for Humanity International. Our purpose was to build as many houses as possible within the two years we were to live in Morata, a crime ridden squatter settlement in Port Moresby.

The house we would be living in was right next to the Pentecostal pastor's house, and fifty yards from the Pentecostal church, as well as the assistant Pentecostal pastor's house. The compound also included a Pentecostal halfway house and a small house for the Pentecostal missionary doctor who visited periodically from Australia.

We arrived by surprise, but no one wanted us there anyway. The former volunteers left a bad taste in everyone's mouth. They didn't get along well with the local committee who directed the project, and the pastor didn't want to deal with another group of expatriates. Dr. Ferguson, the Australian missionary, made arrangements for our arrival, anyway, and we landed in the city described as the "New York of the South Pacific" because of its high crime rate.

Port Moresby was indeed one of the most dangerous cities in the world in which to live. In a way, it was probably proper that Papua New Guinea's capital city be described in such a way. People used superlatives when describing PNG. The mountains were towering and some of the most rugged in the world. Their rugged terrain was punctuated by rushing rivers and plunging ravines. The people were often described as the most isolated and primitive. Occasionally the outside world even discovered a previously unknown tribe in the remote highlands bordering Irian Jaya. PNG did not have big animals but had 250 species of mammals, mostly bats and rodents. It also had the beautiful Birds of Paradise. The orchids were plentiful, and the pink or white blossoms from a frangipani tree filled an entire house with their lovely aroma.

We landed at the Port Moresby airport drenched with perspiration and enthusiasm. This was our first "job" as missionaries, although we didn't feel we fit the title. There were beautiful hills surrounding the airstrip, but what I noticed was the humidity, and how short the Papua

New Guineans were. We arrived past midnight, and the cabbie looked welcoming. He drove us to a hotel by the beach that was cheap and had vacancies. It was too dark to really see the conditions, but we slept well, anxious to get to our new "home". In the morning, we hired the cab again. "Take us to Morata, please." The driver seemed to have an amused expression on his face. He said, "I rarely get calls to Morata."

It took about fifteen minutes to drive through Port Moresby. I was surprised it had tall buildings, stores and offices. We continued the drive out to the suburbs, past the parliamentary buildings, and beautiful flowering trees. I would later go there to pick yellow and orange blossoms to decorate my table.

Our unannounced arrival in Morata was on a Sunday morning, while church services were in progress. We knew the compound had a church, and we could hear it as we drove into the gravel driveway. There were no doors or windows on the church, just open space, and people sat on hard, wooden benches, which were spilling out of the open doorway. As the taxi slowly drove past the church, I tried to look inside. I could see all black people, with one red-haired girl standing with the others. I wondered who she was and if she was American. Then I saw a white man in a bright red shirt walking with his arm around a tall black teenager. The white man was completely engrossed in smiling and talking to the boy. He didn't even notice us, sitting in the taxi cab a few yards down from the church.

Amidst the confusion of our arrival and church being dismissed, it took some time to find the pastor, Charles Lapa. We met several people and told them who we were. They were all surprised that we were in Morata.

Finally, a short Papua New Guinean man with a big Jimmy Carter smile came up to us quickly, and introduced himself as Charles Lapa. We were soon to discover that his influence reached beyond Morata. Charles Lapa could rightfully be called the Billy Graham of Papua New Guinea. He preached in evangelistic crusades throughout PNG, and was especially successful in reaching the rascals. Rascal is the term used for a whole group of individuals from juvenile delinquents to hardened criminals. They epitomized all of the crime and social problems of the country.

Pastor Lapa introduced us to his wife, Lucille. I gave her a warm African hug and then kissed her on the cheek, as I had done with Somalis. I felt her withdraw in embarrassment and took it personally for some time, until I realized that social customs and practices were very much different here than in the other places I had lived.

The keys to our house were missing, so we had to break in. The place hadn't been occupied for a couple of months and was a mess. Gecko turds covered the kitchen cabinets. Dust was thick on the furniture, and a dead toad was in the toilet. We stayed in a guest house in town while our bungalow was cleaned and painted by the ex-rascals living in the adjacent halfway house. These were the boys whom we came to know and love.

Outsiders seldom ventured into Morata. It was known as the home and refuge for rascals, and a dumping ground for stolen cars. Most expatriates were afraid to go near Morata, and few even knew how to find it. I met an Irish lady who had worked with a poverty housing project in England; she was keen to spend some time with us and help on our project, but her husband wouldn't let her come to Morata. A few days after meeting her, a small tribal war broke out in our neighborhood, confirming her husbands' fears. Port Moresby, and especially Morata, sounded like terrible places to live, but there was a good side. From certain parts of the city, the views of Fairfax and Moresby harbors were picturesque. Beaches were always close. The Owen Stanley mountain range and the famous Kakoda Trail were only 30 minutes away from Morata. These mountains have no snow cover, but it was much cooler at several thousand feet, and the vegetation was different than that at sea level.

In many ways our living arrangements were pleasant. Our cottage was on a small rise and open to the soothing, tropical breezes, which were much softer than the harsh, biting wind of Somalia. Our small, front veranda overlooked a field bordered by a creek where children could swim and people would be baptized. In the distance was a large hill covered with palm and banana trees.

The house was plain, but had a washing machine, running water and electricity. We had no hot water, so we often waited until the day warmed up to take our showers. The furniture was functional and casual, a bamboo frame with cushions. The windows were folding slats that cranked open and shut. The geckos took care of any bugs that would get in. The roof wasn't joined tightly against the walls, so geckos could come and go, but this was true of any house in PNG. The floors were bare cement. Given all this, I still yearned for an occasional hot, bubble bath and a plush carpet in which to sink my toes.

We soon gained the acceptance by the people of Morata. As we drove through the streets in an old, dented, white Nissan pick-up truck with our kids sitting in the back, people would wave and smile and call out Master, the Pidgin word for European. Later, that old colonial expression would be changed to Sister Pat and Russell. Then we knew that we were truly residents of Morata.

The church was a major force in the slums of Port Moresby, and Morata was no different in that respect. The frequent services were long, but sitting on a hard wooden bench was forgotten in the spirit and energy of the worship. Sitting in the open-air church with a view of the distant mountains and the blooming bougainvillea all around, I thought, "God must be pleased with these people".

Visiting a relatively new habitat house

Port Moresby, PNG: Laura and friends

CHURCH AND THE JESUS CENTRE

Pat

"Yu mi amamas", clap-clap, "Long Papa God", clap-clap, "Long meri meri belong em" woke me up every morning at 5:30 a.m. The Jesus Centre boys were beginning their morning devotions. I listened to them and prayed silently, then began my morning devotions. This was something new to me, but I guess it started with Tony. Tony was about fourteen years old and had been in the halfway house a couple of years. I don't think he ever committed any serious crimes, but was more of a street urchin, and had no place to stay. With his sad eyes, big ears and smile, Tony was instantly lovable. He was so young and yet got up at 5:30 every morning (along with the other Jesus Centre boys) to spend an hour singing, praying and studying the Bible. He was also expected to attend all of the church services, fast once a week and hold down a full-time job at a local grocery store. I seldom fasted, seldom work up at 5:30 and usually only went to church on Sunday. I thought if a young boy like Tony could be so disciplined and faithful, then I surely could put more effort into my faith. Tony was the impetus that put me on a new spiritual journey of praying and reading the Bible faithfully and fasting.

The Jesus Centre halfway house accommodated thirty boys. The food consisted of tinned fish and rice for dinner and dry biscuits for breakfast and lunch, which was probably better than they would have gotten at home, if they had a home. Most of the boys had only one shirt, and it was usually torn. I would guess who was walking up the road. If it was a green shirt, it was Gilbert. A red shirt would be Morris. Sometimes the boys would trade shirts, and then I would be confused!

The center was managed by an Aussie, Larry George. He was the white man I had seen in the church, talking to the boy. He had been a bank manager at one of the Australian banks when he felt called to give it all up and devote his time, money and energy in helping boys who had been in prison and wanted to change their lives. Through an investment in Australia, he was able to receive an income for himself, but put most of it into the "Jesus Centre". He also lived with the boys in the center.

Some of the boys were on probation for theft or rape, but they had changed their lives by accepting Jesus as their Savior. I could see the peace in their faces and the love in their hearts. Many of the boys played the guitar, and all of their songs were Gospel choruses.

The boys were living in better circumstances than ever before in their lives, and they had hope. At times, however, they looked forlorn, and their surroundings seemed bleak. One day Russ and I were at the Centre, and I particularly noticed the dirt and flies, the institution green walls and the lack of furniture. The boys were sitting on the floor talking or playing the guitar, and Morris was sitting in the corner looking like a lost pup. Larry went over to him and started talking to him and encouraging him. I forgot about the dirt and grime, and realized that this poignant scene of encouragement and brotherly love was the real fullness of life for these boys.

JESUS CENTRE BOYS

Pat

I began visiting the boys at the Jesus Centre regularly. They woke up the whole compound with their singing and guitar playing early in the morning for their devotions. They ate breakfast, then those that had jobs would leave, and the rest would stay and work in the garden.

The building was "L" shaped. As you walked in the screen door, you either had to go right or left. Right was the new addition of the showers and toilets; immediately left was the main living and dining room. As you continued going left, there was a long hall of bedrooms, including Larry's room on one side and his "office" on the other.

At this time the only furniture were bunk beds, a table and phone in the office, and a long table for eating in the living/dining hall. Next to that was a small room for the kitchen, where Larry would cook a stew of tinned fish and rice every night. In the morning and for lunch they had bread, or a hard type of biscuit. I learned later that all of this was donated, so if they got butter or margarine, fine, if not, fine. I would complain to Larry that this was not nutritious enough, but he graciously ignored me.

I decided to help. I could stop by the bakeries on my way to take the kids to school and pick up the bread and biscuits for the Jesus Centre. I could even check with other bakeries to see if they could donate as well, since the Centre always seemed to be short of food. This was the beginning of my learning how to start something with few resources. Wherever I went now, I thought of the "boys" and if this store or company could donate something. At one point I asked Larry if he ever got tired of begging.

I discovered that I could be bold for these kids, where I could not be for something else. I found that if you are excited about something that will come across to the person you are talking to. That person will then want to join you or do what you ask for. I also learned to ask for discounts. I decided one day that the boys needed blankets. Larry didn't think they did, but to me it was cold at night. I bought some blankets and just dumped them in the middle of the room at the Jesus Centre and saw ten happy faces! I was sort of pleased with myself. When I saw Larry come and go, I was disappointed that he didn't stop to thank me. What I found out later was that the ten boys who were present got the blankets and the others were left out.

Stephen

There were many problems when working with youth, especially those with bad behavior, but were now trying to straighten out. Stephen was one. He was young and good looking, but had burglarized and raped women. After he got out of jail, he wanted to change his life around and became a Christian. He was given free reign to testify to groups of people the change in his life. He was very well spoken and seemed very dedicated. However, one night he "backslid", stole a car and did other misdeeds. Against his better judgment, Larry let him back in, but I was furious. After all, I had a teenage daughter in my house and a back-slid, convicted rapist, was not what I wanted next door. I pleaded with Pastor Lapa to not let him back in, but they did. He worked out, although he was now in the background and no longer gave his testimony to large groups of people.

Pastor Lapa had a ministry towards these kids, called "rascals". He held crusades and really focused on these troubled kids. The local newspaper one day had a huge headline on the front page: Pastor Lapa-the Prophet of the Nation. He, along with Larry, was able to get public support for the half way house and the work they were trying to do. He was even able to have the Prime Minister become a Patron of the Jesus Centre. It was the only such center in the whole country.

Stephen was not a problem again while we stayed there, but it was very dangerous work. Larry's life had been threatened many times by boys who had been kicked out of the Centre, or boys who came back drunk, ready for a fight.

Although there was some public support, most people were not enamored of these boys, or the Jesus Centre. They thought once a criminal, always a criminal, and I learned you have to fight for the rights of these boys, as well as educate the public about them. I always wondered, though, why different boys from the same basic background of poverty, could end up differently. Some would turn to crime and others wouldn't.

Thomas

Larry seemed much alone in his work. Whenever I would see the boys, I would try to talk to them. I spent a lot of time in the "living room", chatting with the boys. Occasionally one or two would walk by with only a towel around him, because the living room was between the showers and the bedrooms. I thought nothing of it. One day I saw a boy from Eastern Province, Thomas, walking away from the compound. I knew Russ and Larry had planned for him to volunteer for Habitat that day, as he was showing "good behavior", and they wanted to prepare him for a regular job. I was surprised when I saw him on the street instead of the work site. I rolled the window down on the truck and asked him what was wrong. He was complaining about something at the Jesus Centre, and decided to leave. Through stopping and talking to him, I managed to have him get in the truck and took him to the job site. He stayed at the center and eventually got a good, steady job. Something settled in my spirit that day: that just possibly, I was able to do some good for these young boys.

Tall Gilbert

Tall Gilbert was one of our favorites. We heard he had done something wrong. About a month later, I was standing in front of him at the church when we had communion service. I noticed out of the corner of my eye, he had refused the communion cup. I brazenly whispered asking him why. He just looked down. In hushed whispers we talked back and forth and it seemed to me that he had already asked God for forgiveness and therefore could take the cup, if he so wanted. I waited to see if he drank the cup. He drank the cup. Larry later told me he thought I was too personal with him, but I felt he had renewed his relationship with God, and should no longer feel guilty.

We often used our truck to help Larry and the boys go places for fun or errands. One of the more regretful uses was the time we had to use our truck to carry the coffin for Gilbert's father from the family's home to the grave site. While waiting at the home for the coffin to be loaded onto the truck, I watched the people come and go and all the activity in this, another squatter settlement of Port Moresby. There were many shade trees and a large hill. People walked in the midday sun. One boy used Styrofoam in place of a hat, kept in place with a stick. One woman walked by with a rock in her hand trying to catch up with another woman, with whom she wanted to fight. Three houses down, a man came home drunk and beat up his wife and kids. He left, came back again, yelled and then finally left.

The Jesus Centre boys and Gilbert were all somber. The drunken man was one of his cousins. The other boys probably remembered when they lived around drunks. The grave site was on the side of a hill overlooking the settlement. Several other graves were in the immediate area. They were covered with rocks and sandy pebbles and marked by sticks and handmade crosses. Some scraps of material hung from the homemade pieces of wood surrounding the graves. Standing under a shade tree, Russ, Larry and I waited for the diggers to finish digging a hole big enough for the coffin.

Gilbert's sister was crying, moving her arm to and fro and nodding her head back and forth. No one surrounded her with their warmth or comfort. Gilbert was sitting on the bare earth, weeping, next to his brother, who was also weeping, with a towel wrapped around his eyes, all alone. Before lowering the casket into the ground, it was opened one last time, and the wailing became more intense.

The casket was finally lowered into the ground, and we led Gilbert away. Russ was driving the truck with Gilbert in front. I was sitting in the back of the truck with the halfway house boys and a bunch of children. Simon began to play his guitar, and I asked him to play the sad song that I heard him play several nights earlier. He played the wrong song, but all of the children suddenly joined in singing, and a gloomy day was brightened.

Russ and I tended to go for the underdog, no matter if they were right or wrong. When Larry would kick out a boy, he would usually come to our house, and we would try to work out a solution. But usually Larry was right. I learned a lot from Larry on dealing with these kids. I knew he did not have a counseling background, so I asked him how he knew what to say to the boys. He would often be found in his small bedroom with the door closed, talking, counseling, crying and praying with the boys. He just said the Holy Spirit helped him. Now I could say that too. When I didn't know what to say to a boy who had just done something wrong or to help a boy get back on his feet, I prayed and asked for God's guidance. The lessons I learned in PNG would help me later in different places with different problems.

Port Moresby, PNG: Thomas and Ryan

LIVING IN PORT MORESBY

Pat

I had tried a shot at home-schooling, but our eldest, Laura, needed to be around more friends. We were able to enroll the girls in a Catholic International school, run by Australians. Laura and Katie made friends of people from different countries. The uniforms were brown and white with a white uniform for sports.

Laura was happy to have friends and be around other kids. She also played T-ball and won her first game. Laura enjoyed visiting her friends who lived in the nice parts of town. One of her friends even had a swimming pool.

I volunteered to help with the school's drama club, which had seven kids. One girl wanted to join because she wanted to be a movie star. I had them stretch like cats or be a gorilla chasing a butterfly, which they seemed to enjoy. They are also did a play called "Three Questions", based on a work by Tolstoy. Laura's favorite teacher was originally from India. I enjoyed visiting an Indian women's group. They had a beautiful showing of girls wearing traditional dresses from different parts of India.

Katie got into trouble for talking in class, which was a contrast from the previous year when she hardly talked at all. She was the only white girl in class. The other students were locals, Philippino or Indian. She asked me why there were more black people in the world than white. She made friends, and they were always hugging her and waving to her. Katie liked to make money, even at this age. When her clothes got too small, she wanted to sell them. She and a neighbor friend tried to sell sandwiches at Sunday school. When Katie wanted a piece of paper to draw on, she just pushed the button on the Xerox machine.

Ryan made friends with everybody. When we went to the beach, Ryan ran to the first kid he saw and started playing. Ryan spent much of his time talking and playing with the Jesus Centre boys. He played a lot with Betty Lapa, Pastor Lapa's daughter, running barefoot in the driveway. Russ and the Jesus Centre boys made him toys out of wood, and the boys showed him how to use a sling shot. He cut out circles and called them moons, and cut his own hair in the process.

Every day was different and you never knew what to expect. We enjoyed our times away from work. I attended an International Ladies Tea, where I met about five women married to oil men here, and a few Swedish and Finnish ladies. One Russian lady was having a lively discussion with one of the oil baronesses about changing the people here because of oil. One thought it was positive and the other negative. I also met a Nigerian woman whose husband had a coffee and rubber plantation an hour away. They employed 2000 workers. It was lovely talking to all the international ladies, including the Australians.

We made several attempts to become more fluent in Pidgin. One teacher who was sent to us seemed to be frustrated by our inability to learn quickly. He soon ended up in jail on a traffic offense. A visiting German evangelist announced that God told him to teach us Pidgin. We let him try to teach us, but two days after our first class, he became deathly ill and ended up in a hospital. When he recovered, he left for Australia, but we heard that he ended up in jail for not paying a hotel bill.

One time Russ, Larry and I played tennis with one of Larry's friends who had a tennis court in his back yard. Russ was very happy. He beat both of us! We ended up being invited to the friend's house for dinner the next night. We also enjoyed swimming at hotel pools. Our jobs actually required us to be on call 24 hours a day, so we enjoyed recreational time whenever we got it.

I prayed every morning for wisdom in dealing with the myriad of problems. People showed up at our door with many requests. One man wanted Habitat to pay for his $4,000 college tuition. We had a sad case of a man contemplating suicide, because he had to move his wife and 4 children to nine different houses. We tried to give him hope that things would improve for his family. We also had the usual requests from homeowners for paint or pieces of lumber at all hours of the day.

I planted a rose bush and it flourished, but nothing else grew. I wished I could have successfully grown a frangipani tree with its beautiful aroma. One of our neighbor's puppies kept lying in my lilies, so they pretty much died. We received a surprise package from my sister. She sent a whole bunch of Agatha Christie books, and Russ and Laura read them voraciously.

One day I decided I should get more involved in the church activities, after a sermon in church. Many of the homeowners, the Jesus Centre boys and Habitat volunteers and most of the people we worked with went to this church. I asked if I could start teaching a Sunday school class for the kids. The church agreed. Seventy well-behaved four to six year olds sat in my living room as I told Bible stories and sang songs about Jesus. Some of the older PNG girls would translate for me and be my helper. I had to keep Katie from opening the refrigerator door. She asked Jesus into her heart in class on July 1, 1990. It was hard to keep Ryan sitting still for the class, as he was always moving. The class lasted two hours. I had no teaching materials at first, but I attended a teacher's workshop every night for a week. This provided me with teaching ideas.

I decided to introduce a song called "Up to Zion", which was a very vibrant song. I added some moves to it, which they loved. One thing that surprised me, however, was how difficult it was for the kids to form a circle. We practiced many times in the open field where I tried to get them to hold hands and go in a circle. When the day came to perform in front of the church, the children raised their arms in the air and formed a circle. At this point everyone in church started laughing hysterically. The performance wasn't that funny, and I never understood why the people were laughing. I was just happy that the kids performed as asked.

For Palm Sunday we drove out to the countryside to get palm leaves for the service. I'm glad we brought some locals with us to choose the right trees. The kids enjoyed the palm leaves, and this may have been the first time they learned about Palm Sunday. Each kid colored an Easter egg and most of them had eaten it by the time they returned to their parents.

After church on Easter we went to a club and had a barbecue. The kids had an Easter egg hunt. Most of the people were Chinese with Australian accents, so it was a little funny to see a Chinese Easter bunny. Later we played egg races with some of the church kids and hid the eggs. The day after Easter was a national holiday. Russ played a little bit of baseball with the Jesus Centre boys.

I volunteered to teach a "Religious Instruction" class to elementary kids in one of the nearby national schools. It was a required course, once a week, in all the schools. The Papua New Guinea constitution stipulates that it is a Christian nation.

Sometimes I just wanted a western style church service, so we would go to the Church of the Nazarene in Port Moresby. They had an organ, proper hymn books and an American preacher. One night there was a Scottish guy who played the bag pipes. He then gave a testimony. One night when he and his wife were taking their maid back to her home in the slums of Port Moresby; they were stopped by a gang of boys who started yelling for them to get out of the car. He knew if his maid or wife went out of the car, they would be raped. He went out himself and tried to talk to the boys. Things were escalating when he said, "Stop! In the name of God!", but they continued what they were doing. Then he said, "Stop! In the name of Jesus!", and they immediately stopped! He then drove the maid to her home, and came back later to talk to the boys and gave them Bibles.

We started a Bible Study for the Jesus Centre boys in our home. Russ took a passage from the Bible and listed questions. We broke into smaller groups and answered the questions. We then came back together in a group to discuss them.

I thought it would be a good idea for the Jesus Center boys to serve others. We visited a home for handicapped kids. I had never been here before. It was pretty shocking-kids with no clothes on, and dirt and stench everywhere. I remember thinking I could do anything but bathroom duty. All of a sudden a tall, skinny girl with no clothes on took my hand and took me to the bathroom. I helped her sit on the toilet. It wasn't so bad after all. Meanwhile, some of the guys were praying for the kids, asking for Jesus to heal them.

One night we talked about how good can come out of bad, when someone popped in to tell us the Centre had been broken into. Apparently they had broken in while we they were all in the Bible study! It was only 500 yards away. They stole money, some important papers and clothes from the boys, but couldn't get the TV out of the window! Now the boys had only the shirts on their backs; some were mad at first, but most took it very humbly. We pretty much knew who did it, a former Centre boy who was kicked out. Getting the proof was difficult. The local TV station came and interviewed some of the boys, along with Pastor Lapa and Larry.

One of my favorite times was riding in the back of the pick up truck with the children and driving around Morata. The deeply creviced hill leading to a new settlement area was improved to a graded, bedded road. The two foot ditches in the road became smooth surfaces. Half painted houses and bare cement became neighborhoods in hues of blue, green and white, decorated with palm leaves. Driving through Morata was like being on parade, people smiling and waving. Habitat was really appreciated and welcomed here. Some homeowners were interviewed on the radio, and many said that having a Habitat home helped their marriage. Previously they moved from house to house with no permanent home. One lady said that since getting a Habitat house she stopped smoking and eating betel nut (a stimulant), and now went to church. People even called Russ the "bigpela" man, one who worked hard in the hot sun. Driving through the bowels of Morata, past the dump, and at the top of a hill, the vista of new Habitat homes were cropping up with a backdrop of distant mountains covered by shadowy clouds, giving a different view each time you saw it.

Some fellow Habitat workers from the Solomon Islands visited one time. They took one of the mini buses to our compound, and the other riders were mad when the driver went out of his way to drop them off. The driver told the passengers, "These people are from Habitat. They help us, so we can help them".

Some evenings we sat on the stoop watching the beautiful sunsets by the mountains, with wisps of smoke circling up and disappearing in the sky. Everything is green. People start little brush fires, so there was hazy smoke in the air.

It could be dangerous at night. Curfews in Port Moresby were common. A boy was shot by the police in Morata. One evening we were visiting another church down the road in Waigani. All of a sudden, "rascals" jumped out of nowhere and started yelling. The people were scared to death; some started speaking in tongues, another was holding a plate to throw at them, while one of the Pastors from our church grabbed his kids and forgot about his wife! Then all of a sudden they took their masks off. They were the Jesus Centre boys, putting on a "drama"! Needless to say, no one was amused.

In our cell group, I asked the boys to name a person significant in their lives that was encouraging or helped them grow spiritually. I began by talking about Tony, the Jesus Centre boy, and how he had encouraged me. I said that people encourage by taking the time to talk to them, or share Scripture verses, or was an example. I told them the story of Moses in Exodus 17 and how his friends had lifted Moses' hand to help him in his time of need. Homework was to pick a person you would not normally speak to and share time with them. I then had them go into groups of pairs and told to share something they hadn't confessed to before, and then pray for each other. I and two other Jesus Centre boys had similar problem of anger and unforgiveness. It felt better after just confessing my anger towards certain people.

I spent some time trying to beautify our home. The floor was painted and needed fresh paint, so I would try to do a piece at a time, in green. The Jesus Centre boys helped paint the outside walls and chairs. The window slats were always open to let in the cool breezes coming across the field, but also brought dust. I loved to go to the different areas close by where frangipani flowers were blooming, and would cut a few to have in our home. Their smell was intoxicatingly sweet.

One Saturday I delivered a rocking chair to a pregnant American woman, who was married to a Papua New Guinean. I took a couple of Jesus Centre boys with me and they carried the rocking chair to the door. I knocked, and Sally opened the door, with only a skirt on. This was common among the locals, but not Americans. I tried not to look shocked. We only stayed a little while. I then went to the Steamships store to get something for Russ. When I got home, I went to the pool with Russ and the kids. We then had dinner at our favorite pizza place, and Katie fell asleep on the chair. Back home, we played scrabble with one of the Jesus Centre boys and then argued about the gifts of the Spirit.

On Sunday, St. Patrick's Day, I read the day's lesson at 6:00 am, fixed breakfast, ironed, picked up dirty clothes and cleaned the house. I went to the church service and sat with two Papua New Guinea friends, Susan and Nancy. We gossiped and then the preacher talked about women in the back of the church gossiping! He said they should be gossiping about Jesus. True. After church a bunch of Sunday School kids ran up to me and hugged me. Katie tried to make a St. Patty's Day card, but got frustrated. Russ took the kids to the store. I went back to church's evening service which was early because of the curfew.

The Woman Who Never Spoke

She was sitting on my front porch one day when I came home. I said, "Hello?" She didn't respond, but just looked down at her foot. I looked down at her foot and saw a huge hole with blood and pus coming out. I didn't even know where to take her. I motioned to the car and she pointed this way and that until I had dropped her off at a nearby clinic.

Two days later she was back, sitting on my front porch. Her foot was neatly bandaged and she was smiling. She stayed on my porch for hours, never speaking. A couple of times her husband came. He said she had demons in her. She was called the "long long lady". I asked him if he wanted us to pray for her. I stopped painting the floor, and got Larry at the church. One other person I saw first said he'd pray, but then changed his mind because he was scared. I was too. Her husband said she was the happiest twelve years ago, a year after the birth of their first born when she went back to her village. I told the story about the woman who had been sick for twelve years and how she had touched Jesus' garment and was healed. Larry prayed for the spirit of asthma and curse to leave her. I told her husband God will answer his prayer because he had been so faithful and loving to her. Her small kids came and sat with her. When it got dark, her husband came and took her home. I still didn't know her name.

One day she was standing at our church building. People came running to tell me she had hit the pastor. I ran and found a crowd of men ready to beat her. Someone knew where she lived, so we walked her home. Her husband invited me back to her wooden house on stilts. He showed me the "bilum" (bag) she was knitting, just for me. She had never knitted before. She still didn't speak, but she showed love to her children. Her husband showed love most of all, to her. He never yelled at her or hit her, but one day I went to visit her and she was gone. Her husband had sent her back to her village. She had tried to set the house on fire. I was sad. Years later I thought she probably had Alzheimer's disease.

Port Moresby, PNG Kids in our truck

Port Moresby, PNG: Russ and Katie

THE BAREFOOT DOCTOR

Pat

Shortly after our arrival in Port Moresby, some American friends who had been in PNG for some time came down from the highlands (the mountainous areas inland) for a visit.

They wanted us to meet a good friend who had been helpful to them. Her name was Dr. Lee, and she had an office in one of the shopping districts. I pictured Dr. Lee to be a short, little Chinese lady with black hair wrapped in a bun. When we stopped at the office to see her, she was not in, so we left a message.

A few days later a minibus, with an old logo scraped off, roared to the front of our house. It looked like a 1960's hippie van. There were several Papua New Guineans in the van, but a lady with long brown hair and soft brown eyes stepped out of the van, barefoot.

"Hello, I'm Rosemary Lee. I'm sorry I missed you." I was stunned! She was Australian not Chinese, and she was barefoot. I tried not to act too surprised as I invited her inside. She was so open, friendly and accepting to us, strangers from America.

Rosemary invited us to tea and made arrangements to pick us up, but didn't specify what time. Three o'clock came and went. By five o'clock I started to fix dinner. Just after finishing the dishes, Rosemary pulled in at seven o'clock and asked, "Are you ready?" We weren't sure what we were ready for, but we piled into her van. It was about a mile to her home. The driveway was full of different types of vehicles: an old Land Rover, a late model sedan, an old pick-up and the minibus. Two dogs greeted us and several cats were resting on the porch. A multi-colored parrot was perched in an oversized cage that hung from one of the many palm trees and was squawking at the other birds.

Rosemary opened the door, and I saw a number of Papua New Guineans sitting around the airy living room watching TV, or playing with her two year old son, Jeffrey. An elderly man stood up, smiled and left the room. "We'll be ready in a few minutes." Rosemary said from the open kitchen. I could see her preparing platters of vegetables and fruit with Tawa, her PNG sister-in-law. Tawa looked like a girl right out of a Gauguin painting with her long, velvety black hair and large, soulful eyes. She was quiet and indispensable to Rosemary, either cooking and cleaning, or caring for Jeffrey when Rosemary was working.

It eventually occurred to me that we were not to have "tea", but dinner, and quite a dinner it was. The center piece was a platter of every type of tropical fruit available in this part of Oceania. The rice and chicken were served with various types of vegetables and sauces. Rosemary opened a coconut, and the children had their first taste of coconut milk. Ryan grew to love coconuts in Papua New Guinea. Even though we were full from our previous "tea", we ate as much as we could. Rosemary's husband, Rex, was in Canada studying for a second degree, but Rosemary had plenty of company. The house was always full of "wantoks". Wantoks are people from the same tribe that speak the same language; in this case, it refered to Rosemary's extended family. The children were allowed to do as they liked, and enjoyed the freedom of her house. As Katie said, "We never got into trouble at her house".

As well as being a medical doctor, Rosemary doctored sick animals. While we were there, a bandaged rabbit was romping around the living room. Before we left, Rosemary said we should bring our family medical problems to her, which we did.

Rosemary's parents were missionaries in India. She had three sisters, and they all became doctors. Rosemary not only treated our family medical problems, but also the Jesus Centre boys in the halfway house. When we later became friends some Somali refugees, Rosemary took care of their health problems. One time when I was bedridden with something that felt like malaria, Rosemary visited each day. One morning I woke up to find her ironing my laundry, barefoot of course.

Rosemary became my best friend and confident, and she would listen as I aired my grievances, sometimes about PNG. She would then suggest a new place to discover or visit. We would go to lunch or take Ryan and her son Jeffrey on an outing, and I would feel revived. We put our sons in the same pre-school.

Rosemary introduced us to the beauty of Papua New Guinea, such as Sogeri Mountain. It took a windy and dangerous road to get there in order to see the lush greenery and rushing rivers.

We introduced Rosemary to the Cathay Club. It was a swimming and sports club run by the Chinese, originally formed because the whites kept the Chinese out of their clubs. The place had the ambiance of a rundown, 1950's California motel, but it was inexpensive and they had a swimming pool. It was one of our getaways from the demands of Morata. Even Russ enjoyed sneaking off for an afternoon swim.

Rosemary and I started taking aerobics classes. I bought Rosemary a new leotard outfit and found out that she was pregnant. The pregnancy didn't slow her down, and she didn't even seem to have morning sickness. Toward the end of her pregnancy, she and I went out to lunch. I didn't see her for a couple of days, and then one evening I pulled up the driveway, and there was Rex and Rosemary holding their newborn baby girl at our doorstep. Rosemary had delivered that morning and was up and around visiting her friends. The baby's Papua name was Puwana. Rosemary was happy to have a girl in the household.

One day I read a small article in a newspaper describing depression and feeling like nothing mattered. I showed it to Rosemary and told her that was how I felt. She immediately had me talk to someone, which helped. Papua New Guinea was supposed to be a Christian country, but they had Pori Pori, which was voodoo type stuff, as well as ancestor worship.

RASCALS, TRIBAL WARS AND HOUSES

Russ

I first met Billy when he approached us to ask that we use the boys from his youth club to help build houses. I had watched them play rugby in the field in front of our house almost every day, rain or shine. Some were very young, and they were much like the boys in the halfway house. We had just started building houses in a new section of Morata where the city had made lots available for low cost housing. We decided to give Billy and his boys a chance, so we assigned them to a lot, gave them the necessary tools and material and told them to build a house. Billy knew what he was doing with respect to building a house and supervising the boys. Their house was the first one completed in this new section of Morata. The boys were tough, but they respected Billy and worked hard.

When we started making bricks rather than buying cement blocks for the houses, we recruited Billy's boys to dig the clay and make the bricks. The boys were proud of the work they were doing. It gave them respect, and the little bit of pocket money that they received, helped their families, and, together with the hard work, kept the boys out of trouble. Billy soon became our chief volunteer and supervised all of the construction work for the project. A bit of rivalry soon developed between me and the Habitat boys and Pat and the Jesus Centre boys.

An amusing incident happened shortly after we recruited the boys to make bricks. Pastor Lapa decided to hold a meeting of all the rascals in the area to talk and have a barbecue. We sat on our veranda that evening to see what these rascals looked like. One after another we recognized them as our Habitat volunteers. We knew, however, that these boys were no longer rascals but rather hard working citizens serving their community. We would continue to sit on our veranda and watch the boys play rugby, but knowing that they now had a purpose in life. Our motto was: "Make them sweat, give them lunch and get them saved."

The house building project received quite a bit of publicity. The new American Ambassador visited and was genuinely interested in the work that was going on in Morata, and how building low cost houses and putting youth to work was answering some major social problems. The Prime Minister of Papua New Guinea, Rabbie Namilieu, presented the keystone speech at the dedication ceremony for a recently completed group of homes. When a house was completed, and the family was ready to move in, we would have a dedication ceremony and present the homeowner with a Bible. This group of homes was completed at about the same time, and this group of homeowners was a particularly hardworking and dedicated group. The homeowner's sweat equity is a key part of the Habitat program. Some homeowners did most of the work themselves and others needed help from our volunteers. Several of the families who had a row of houses together were Pangis. They were from a village called Pangia in the Southern Highlands. I always called their neighborhood New Pangia and used their houses as models when giving tours to visitors.

We ended up building 33 houses in Morata. This group was among our first and fun to build. Later houses were built with pressed bricks and that was an innovative and interesting community project. The houses were a simple 6 meter x 6 meter concrete or brick square with two bedrooms and a tin roof. It had a small porch in front and some had a toilet area in the back. The homeowners arranged the cooking area in any way they preferred.

One evening Billy and I were sitting in the garage, drinking coffee and talking over the day's progress, when one of the boys ran up and said that James Kari was drunk and had stolen some cement and roofing iron from one of the construction sites. James was a friend of ours, a Habitat homeowner and Billy's brother-in-law. I felt betrayed, got mad and hopped in the truck with Billy and headed to James' house. It occurred to me that the Bible advises against listening to fools or following angry men, and here was Billy following an angry man. When we got to James' house, we found the cement and roofing on the ground and James standing in the doorway. I started grabbing roofing iron to put it in the truck, but it was too bulky to handle. I said to James, "Help me put this in the truck. What are you trying to prove?" James was drunk and started complaining that he had done a lot for us, and he needed the roofing iron and should have it. Billy grabbed a bag of cement, and James attacked him. Billy grabbed a tree limb and hit James on the head. James' wife and a couple of his Wantoks held James back. I grabbed Billy so we could get in the truck before James and Billy killed each other. James broke loose, hurled a brick at the truck and broke the windshield as we made our escape.

Back at my house, Billy and I were discussing what happened and how James stole the building materials. Pretty soon, James and his ugly, purple truck appeared in the driveway. James got out of the truck and started hurling insults and throwing beer bottles at me. Pat later said she liked the way I stood my ground but didn't fight. I reminded her that James was the equivalent of a golden gloves champion, and I wasn't about to fight him. The commotion drew a large crowd. Onlookers circled the driveway outside of our house with James in the center ranting and raving and occasionally throwing beer bottle at someone. Then out of the crowd, Billy's wife charged at James with an axe in her hand and shouting in their tok ples (tribal language) that James was a scumbag. Billy had to restrain his wife, and someone dragged James into his truck and took him home. It was quite an exciting evening, but it wasn't over yet.

It started getting dark. The crowd had dispersed. We were thinking about going to bed, when we heard a truck pull up outside of the house. It was James again, and he had a bush knife in his hand. He kept saying, "Come out Russ, I want to talk to you". I talked to him through the window, but didn't consider going outside to talk to a drunken James Kari who was brandishing a bush knife. He kept wandering around outside, and I kept talking to him through the window. I decided to call the police but couldn't get through, so I called Rex, Rosemary Lee's husband. Rex soon arrived and started talking to James. James seemed to be sobering up a bit, and Rex was able to reason with him. Rex convinced James to go home, and after he left, we all sat outside again and discussed the night's events. A police car pulled up shortly and asked what happened and if we wanted to press charges. We said it was a family matter, and we could take care of it.

Two nights later, I saw James drive down the road with a bunch of his wantoks in the back of the truck. I smelled trouble and asked my Pangi friend with whom I was talking to get his wantoks and stand by. James showed up a little later, but he was sober and apologetic. We had a long talk and patched things up, and then James got into the truck with his Karema wantoks and the Pangis, and drove off toward New Pangia. We remained friendly with James thereafter, but the trust was gone, and he wasn't the friend that he once was.

Drunkenness is a major problem in Papua New Guinea. If alcohol were banned, half of the country's social problems would disappear. I think, however, that tribal warfare would remain. Any small conflict between two individuals, such as tripping during a soccer game or talking to a girl, can easily escalate into a tribal war. One time we ended up with a completed house, but the homeowner abandoned his claim to the house and went back to his village. We met some business people who wanted to buy a house for one of their employees. They offered twice the construction cost, so we thought it was wise to sell it and build two houses with the proceeds. On the day we were to show the house, I was driving the prospective buyers from our compound to the housing site and ran headlong into a group of at least one hundred Sepik men with bows and arrows and wearing feathers and war paint. These were the same people that I saw every day going to work in regular clothes, and some were friends. Today, however, they were at war with another tribe, and they advised us to turn around and go back. We took the back road to the housing site, where we had to park the truck and ford a stream. The people saw the house and seemed pleased, but we never heard from them again.

One time I was delivering timber to a construction site, and ran into a group of men from the Eastern Highlands. They were standing next to a burned-out car, and some were carrying spears. I asked what happened, and they said the Pangis torched the car. I delivered the timber and was returning home up another road on a hill where I ran into the Pangis. The Pangis said they got into a fight with the Gorokas (the main town in the Eastern Highlands) during a soccer match, and the Gorokas burned down one of their houses, so they torched a Goroka car. Both groups agreed not to destroy any of the houses that we were building, and eventually the old men of each tribe got together and settled the matter.

Most conflicts in Papua New Guinea are settled by payback or compensation. If someone from one tribe kills someone or destroys something from another tribe, the offended tribe either kills or destroys in a like manner or receives some sort of payment from the other tribe as compensation for the loss. In many conflicts, however, the retribution is escalated on both sides until there is a tragic loss of life and property. This complicates the peace settlement and negotiations on compensation. In Morata, if one tribe did something particularly offensive, the other tribes would team-up and run them out of the settlement. The exiled tribe's return would be a drawn out and complicated affair.

Tribal allegiances are geographic. For instance, the Pangies are from Pangia, and the Chimbus are from Chimbu Provence. This makes it simple for the outsider, but in reality, the tribal allegiance is to a person's tok ples, which can be a very small village or a larger area where everyone speaks the same tribal language. Extended family members are required to share and help each other.

Habitat houses under construction in squatter settlement of Moratta

New house dedication

Lady watching her habitat house being built in the highlands

Papua New Guinea Sing Sing: A Highlands welcome

WORK CAMP IN MOROBE PROVINCE

Pat

I should have known that things would not go as planned, when I arrived at the Lae Airport and no one was there to meet me. I was there to help with a Global Village Work Camp, sponsored by Habitat, in a village about two hours from Lae, Papua New Guinea. The town of Lae is more pleasant than Port Moresby. There are plenty of shade trees, and the open areas are grassy with many flowers. I found my Morobe Province Habitat counterparts, who were hosting the work camp. They had arranged for accommodations that night at a clean, cheery guest house. I met the other work campers that night who were mostly young, male Australians. We practiced singing in Pidgin, and talked about the anticipated adventure in the New Guinea Highlands.

The next morning we boarded a bus with open sides for the two hour drive to the village of Timibing. The road was smooth and paved for half the trip, then we turned right to go straight up a mountain. The landscape was green and lush, and a beautiful river coursed along the side of the mountain. The road, however, was practically eroded and blocked by landslides which made negotiating the hairpin turns a heart-pounding affair.

We stopped to pick up some local villagers who were coming to help with the work camp. It was a bit stuffy in the bus, even with open sides, and I began feeling sick. Luckily we soon stopped just short of our destination to give the villagers more time to prepare the welcoming ceremony. I was able to walk around and smell the fresh mountain air and eat a banana. Now I was ready for a proper arrival.

The welcoming ceremony would be a "sing sing". A "sing sing" is a dance or drama performed in full traditional dress and make –up. As we walked up a path toward the host village, we heard an ear piercing cry by the village women. We looked ahead on the path and there they stood with war paint, grass skirts, feathers and spears. Two men with bamboo poles held us back, while the women were joined by the men in a wild dance of hooping and hollering and spear throwing. This was a war dance, and two men played the part of victims with pig blood smeared on their bodies. The beating drums, the women wailing, the masks and the spears had an unnerving effect. If this was their greeting to friends, how would they greet enemies? When the dancing was over we all shook hands. The villagers explained that they used to fight that way, but now they were Christians and quit fighting. I don't think I believed them.

The village was beautiful with a nearby stream running down the mountain, and neat little houses with thatched roofs and tall, yellow and orange flowers. We ate lunch in an open area on rough-cut benches and tables. The women of the village used huge banana leaves as tablecloths. Our menu consisted primarily of rice and green, leafy vegetables that flavored the bland taro, a variety of potatoes. We slept in a newly constructed house with mattresses spread on the floor.

The women and men took turns bathing communally in a mountain stream, with our clothes on. Water was redirected through a bamboo pole as a shower. It was refreshing at the end of a hard day to wash my hair in the shower. We washed our clothes and pots and pans in a big area where a pool had formed. One day I joined the other women for a bath in the river. The current was so fast that I lost my bar of soap as well as a borrowed one. One lady was not too keen to loan me her French perfumed soap. The PNG women were not modest, exposing their breasts. They bathed topless in clear view of other people passing by. They also fully exposed their breasts while nursing their babies in church. It seemed to be socially unacceptable, however, for women to expose their thighs.

I was sick for much of the time in Timibing and didn't have a chance to work at building houses. It was a good opportunity however, to sample rural village life, and living a new experience with an energetic group of Australian volunteers was great fun.

On the day we were to leave, the truck didn't make it up the road. That same long, twisting road that seemed so hard to negotiate on our arrival was even longer and more rugged on foot. A recent storm had felled trees onto our path and washed out the roadway. We had to walk carrying our suitcases over and under trees and through debris. I felt weak, and every part of my body ached. I stepped on a rock and fell on my back. Peter, our friend from Chimbu Province, helped me up and carried my bag the rest of the way down the hill. Suddenly there appeared juicy cuts of fresh pineapple. We stopped to savor this delight. The sun didn't seem so hot after that. When we reached the tarmac road and saw the waiting truck, I almost collapsed in exhaustion. It was good to get back to Morata and my own bed, where I could recover from the resulting malaria, dysentery and sore feet.

FIRST CHRISTMAS IN PORT MORESBY

Pat

I came upon him unexpectedly, having run into the fanciest "mall" in town to escape the heat and humidity. As I was passing an Australian-run store with a "snow covered" Christmas tree out front, I saw a short black man wearing a red and white Santa suit. Standing with him were two older men and a woman, looking solemn and serious. They were having their picture taken with Santa. The children were standing at a distance. I waited for the children to go up next, but instead, two other adults took their place to have their picture with Santa. I wondered why the children were not having their picture taken.

The boys in the half-way house were having a traditional "muumuu" for Christmas dinner and invited us. A "muumuu" is a feast in which a whole pig is cooked in the ground. The pig and some vegetables are placed in a hole in the ground and then covered with banana leaves and hot rocks. The pig is cooked all day. Fruit and rice are added to the main course and laid out on banana leaves for a buffet.

Rather than eating with the boys, we had a "traditional" English dinner of roast beef, potatoes, plum pudding and pie. It was quiet around the dinner table, but we could hear all of the commotion outside where the muumuu was being prepared. We washed the dishes, put away the plates, watched the kids play with their toys and sat. There was an unspoken feeling in the air. I think we all secretly wished that we had joined the boys for a Christmas dinner, cooked in the ground.

I don't remember the gifts we exchanged that Christmas, but I do remember the night we went caroling. It was a Christmas Eve service at church. The congregation had brought candles, and Russ and Larry were at the front of the church leading in the singing of Christmas carols. Most of the congregation couldn't read, and many couldn't speak English; but they picked up the carols quickly, especially the choruses.

We helped light each other's candles and moved en masse through the squatter settlement of Morata, singing the congregation's favorite song, "We Wish You a Merry Christmas", with kids and dogs following. Morata had never seen anything like this before. The people spent most of their time outside, because the houses were small and hot. We received stares, smiles and even some thrown beer cans, as we passed the outdoor beer joint and pool hall. Many joined us even if they didn't know the songs.

The group spread out as it moved down the dirt road. The people in the back were eventually singing different carols then the ones in the front. We came to the end of the road where we regrouped and headed back toward the church. There were more socializing and greeting neighbors than singing. By this time, the candles had burnt out but the ebullience remained. It turned out to be a real community event, a night to remember in Morata for all.

SOMALIS IN PORT MORESBY?

Pat

I was stunned to see a picture of Somalis on the front page of the local newspaper. Why and how did they get here? This is about as far away from Somalia as you can get, geographically and socially. In PNG, the pig is the symbol of wealth. In Somalia, the camel is the symbol of wealth and the pig is scorned. In PNG, women breast feed their babies in church. Somali woman covered themselves up and were 99 %Muslim.

After I caught my breath, I looked at the paper again. The headline said, "Somalis Protesting". They were on a hunger strike in front of the Australian Embassy, due to the lack of help from the United Nations while they were living in PNG, and also to help them migrate to Australia. I quickly showed the newspaper to Russ and hurried down to the Australian Embassy to see if I could catch them. My heart was racing as fast as the truck was.

By the time I arrived, they had left. I said to the woman in the office, "I saw Somalis on the front page of the newspaper. Do you know where they are now?" The woman at the Information Desk said, "They were on their way to the United Nations office." I rushed downtown and asked for directions to the U.N. office. Once I found the building and a parking space, I raced up to the office and saw them in the corridor. They were quietly talking to the lady in charge. I was smiling ear to ear. "Are you Somalis? What are you doing here? Where do you live?" Some of them turned around and spoke English. They greeted me, and explained, "We want visas and asylum in Australia." There were three families living together. The men were leaving for Australia soon, and would send for their families when the Australian government let them in.

The Somalis were refreshing: very open, loud, and laughed a great deal in spite of their hardships. Their children laughed and sang. Taking the Somalis under my wing was my respite from Morata. I visited them in their home and had tea (chai) with them. They told me their stories. They thought if they could reach PNG, they would have a good chance of getting into Australia. They came to PNG by way of the Middle East and Malaysia. They said there were Somalis everywhere in the world, including China and Russia, to escape the civil war in their country.

I brought them basic food stuffs, flour and sugar, and took them to the beaches so the kids could have fun and the women could take their minds off their problems. They waded in the water fully clothed. The men in the family were able to make their way to a detention camp in Australia to await their asylum hearing. I saw the women frequently and sometimes brought them to Morata. I loved being with the Somali women and children. A couple of Somali guys who were travelling with the family came to Morata from time to time to talk to Russ. They usually talked about clans and Somali politics.

I talked to the women about Jesus, and how He loved them. I also gave them a Somali Bible. They had some curiosity, but didn't ask many questions. Being with them was a change from my usual routine and I loved revisiting people and things of Somalia.

I found out that the church was going to show live coverage of a Billy Graham Crusade in Asia, on an outdoor T.V. screen at the church. I invited the Somali ladies to join us.

As I was sitting and waiting in the dark for the Crusade to begin, I saw four Somali women walking in their beautiful clothes up the driveway to the church! They joined me on the hard benches sitting outside. We watched the Crusade as Billy Graham preached and gave the final invitation. As we were watching, I wondered what they were thinking.

Afterwards, I invited them over to my house for tea. As they were coming in, Titus from the Jesus Centre slipped in behind them. I had noticed Titus when I attended the 5:30 am devotions at the half way house. A lot of the boys were slumped over or asleep. Titus was standing up, his eyes closed, singing and praying with tears coming down. So when he walked in, I was surprised but very pleased.

I began by asking the ladies what they thought of the film. They said they liked it. All of a sudden, Titus started quoting Scripture after Scripture. I thought maybe this was too much, or too fast, but they kept listening and he kept quoting Scripture. Behold, I stand at the door, and knock: if any man hear my voice, and open the door, I will come in to him, and will sup with him, and he with me." (Revelation 3:20)*. Again in 1 John 1:9, If we confess our sins, He is faithful and just to forgive us our sins, and to cleanse us from all unrighteousness. John 3:16, the most quoted and beloved of all the verses, For God so loved the world that He gave His only begotten Son, that whosoever believeth in Him, should not perish, but have everlasting life. They seemed to understand the basic Gospel message that Jesus died for us and arose, so we could have eternal life if we believed. I heard myself ask, "Would you like to ask Jesus into your heart?" I asked each one, and they said yes, one by one. Titus continued to quote Scripture. We talked some more, and I asked them again; I wanted to make sure they understood what they were doing. They all said yes again. Titus then led them in the sinner's prayer; one by one, they accepted. They seemed happy. I was happy. Titus didn't show much emotion. I went to bed that night praising God for what He had done.

The next day my favorite lady called me. She had called her father in Australia to tell him she had become a Christian. The fact that she told someone confirmed to me that she had really meant it. I knew her father would be furious. In fact, her father threatened to kill her with a knife if she came to Australia as a Christian. This is a typical reaction of Somalis when they find out someone has accepted Jesus.

We wondered if they had sincerely believed. I thought they had, but Titus wasn't sure. Later that night Titus had a dream that confirmed the women were sincere. A few months later, they all received permission to enter Australia. I was heartbroken and shed many tears at the airport. We kept up correspondence for a while, but I hope someday to be able to see them again.

*All Scripture references are from the King James Version

Port Moresby, PNG: Somalis at the beach

EXPECT THE UNEXPECTED

Russ

"Expect the Unexpected" is the motto for Papua New Guinea. Most of our surprises were positive. We received land on which to build houses at a time when the availability of lots was drying up in Morata. We made friends and found helpers in unlikely places. We also found that we could work with Pentecostals. Some of our surprises, naturally, were not so good.

Late one night, after being in Port Moresby for a short time, I gave a visiting English preacher a ride home. This was after a Bible study in our house with the boys from the halfway house. Usually I would have had a truck full of boys going along for the ride, but tonight they were occupied with some other activity, or finishing the dessert. The preacher was staying in someone's house between Morata and a major shopping area, just off the main road.

I dropped the preacher off and was heading back, but I missed the turn-off to the main road. I pulled over a little and prepared to make a U-turn, when I spotted a headlight in my rearview mirror. I waited a bit for what I thought was a motorcycle to pass. The next thing I heard was a crunch, and I felt the car rock. In a split instant I realized that a truck had smashed into my side, and thought, "Great, now I have to deal with some stupid drunk". I focused on the passenger window of the truck that just hit me. My eyes met a glaring, full-bearded, ugly brute that was waving a six inch barreled, .357 magnum Smith and Wesson at me. As I was thinking "Lord, what I am doing here", I spotted, from the corner of my eye, another man getting out of the back of the double cab pick-up. This one had a shotgun. Not wanting to be a victim, I did the only thing I could do – popped the clutch. By the grace of God, the wheel wells didn't lock, and I didn't catch the other truck's bumper. The rear tires spewed stones for what seemed like an eternity, and finally hit the tarmac with an ear piercing whine. The truck fishtailed wildly for a second. I firmly gripped the steering wheel and ducked my head anticipating a bullet through the rear window. I was praying like a Pentecostal, and my dependable, gray workhorse gripped the road and sped off. I didn't dare to peek too soon, but I left the bad guys in the middle of the road with the fool with the shotgun half in the truck and half out. I wondered why they didn't take a passing shot at my truck, but later found out that many criminals carry stolen weapons but few bullets. Thankfully, they didn't want to waste a bullet on my fleeing truck. Pat thought I was making up the story as an alibi for being late. Then she saw the side of the truck.

I had a number of pleasant trips outside of Port Moresby to visit people who wanted to start a Habitat project. Fergusson Island is the middle of three big islands off the tip of the mainland of Milne Bay. The first stop on the way to the islands was Alotau, the provincial capital of Milne Bay. Alotau was clean, peaceful and boring but a nice change to Port Moresby, and specifically Morata. Milne Bay had an interesting history for an apparent insignificant part of the world. Captain John Moresby found this deep, sheltered harbor in 1873 and claimed the entire area for Queen Victoria. The queen must not have been impressed, because she repudiated the claim. Many of the air battles of the Battle of the Coral Sea in World War II took place over the islands and the mainland of Milne Bay. After that historic battle, the Japanese attempted a landing on Milne Bay but were repulsed by Australian troops.

Fergusson Island is flanked by Goodenough Island and Normanby Island. Papua New Guinea's famous third-level air travel to isolated airstrips in rugged terrain was at its most dramatic on these islands off the tip of the mainland. On the flight from Alotau to Salamo, the major settlement on Fergusson Island, the first stop was Esa'ala on Normanby Island. These islands were volcanic mountains rising out of the ocean and covered with lush, green vegetation and thick forests. The airplane descended to within yards of the cresting ocean waves and appeared to set a course that would slam us into the side of the mountain. As the details of the rugged terrain and the facial features of the people on the ground became far too clear, the airplane banked hard to the left. There, carved in the forest a couple of hundred feet above sea level, was a grass airstrip. Bordered on all sides by jungle and tall trees, the margin for error at take-off and landing was probably about the same as for landing on an aircraft carrier.

The landing at Salamo was tame by comparison. The terrain wasn't as mountainous, and a bigger area was cleared for the airstrip. I received a warm welcome and accommodations by the folks at the Methodist Mission. I then made preparations for the trip to a small village that I was to visit. I discovered that the village was on the other side of the island, and the only way to get there was by boat. I hired a 16 foot, wooden boat with a 25 horsepower motor, and the next morning, two local guys and I left for the four hour trip. The sea was calm that morning, and the light breeze was at our advantage. The coastline of the island varied with white, sandy beaches interspersed with rocky shorelines and tangled mangroves reaching to the water's edge. Inhabitants of the idyllic villages along the shore waved and beckoned us to stop for a visit.

We made our destination with time to spare. The village had a school and a health officer but seldom saw outsiders. While talking to the lone government official of the area, I looked over my shoulder and saw two women dressed only in grass skirts. When I looked in their direction, they giggled and ducked behind a tree. As I continued my discussion with the local official, I would look out of the corner of my eye and see the ladies peeking from behind a tree. As they built up the courage to come out of hiding, I would look in their direction, and again, they giggled and ducked behind a tree. This must have been what every explorer or shipwrecked sailor experienced when landing on an uncharted island. This place was on the map, but nobody ever came here.

The return trip wasn't so calm. We had plenty of time to get back to Salamo, but the clouds were building out over the open seas. A few miles down the coast, the rain started falling lightly. As we hit a large gulf and set a course from land tip to land tip, the storm hit as we were traversing deep sea. The waves built to a tumult, and the rain and wind drenched and chilled us. The boat was tossed about, and we had to bail water from the stern. Several waves almost tipped the boat, and I was praying like a Pentecostal again.

My companions were working hard to hit the waves at the proper angle to avoid swamping the boat, and I was trying to stay out of the way and bail water. The worst of the storm hit when we were in the deepest water. As we approached closer to the shoreline, the storm settled to a nice steady rain. The rest of the trip was miserably wet, but we were happy to be out of the storm.

These islands, known as the D'Entrecastaux Group, are mountains rising out of the sea. As such, they would best be described as awe inspiring rather than idyllic. Standing on the shore of one of these islands is like being trapped between two monsters, the mountain and the sea. Sailing the straits between Fergusson and Goodenough gave the person the impression that the only things existing in the world were the sea, the sky and these two magnificent monoliths.

The Sepik River is the Mecca for anyone wanting to study strange cultures and primitive people. The river is a channel of communication into the most remote and foreboding parts of Papua New Guinea. It is also the cultural and artistic hotbed of the country. I came to the Sepik Province not to visit the river but rather a little island off the provincial capital of Wewak, called Kairiru. The boat ride from Wewak to Kairiru was short and pleasant. Dolphins escorted the boat as we circled Mushu Island which stands between the mainland and Kairiru. The rich and varied shades of green and aquamarine were the most beautiful that I had seen in any of the coral atolls of the Pacific or Indian Oceans.

As we approached the island, my companions said to be ready for the traditional greeting that the old man of the village was going to give us. The old man was in traditional dress of grass and beads, and threw red berries at the boat as we pulled up to shore. Later the old man changed his clothes and joined our meetings. I found out that he was my age. This was when I began to realize that, in the Third World, people my age were tribal elders. This village was the location for the school that served the entire island. I was asked to speak to the students, and I described some of the things of America that I thought would be the strangest to them, such as skyscrapers and six lane highways. The students asked some probing questions about American culture, and particularly racial relations. Life on this island seemed tranquil but not as isolated as the islands off Milne Bay.

"Land of Contrasts" is an overused moniker, but it applied to PNG. The beauty and danger existed in a strange harmony unlike any other place on Earth. As much as we loved Papua New Guinea and the people we came to know, it was time to leave. Habitat was having some financial problems that we thought might affect our project. We hurried up the process to turn the project over to the local committee.

Furthermore, a civil war had broken out in Somalia plunging that country into anarchy and chaos. Somalia was being destroyed and people were dying. We had to get there.

The day we left, Pastor Lapa's wife came to our door with some of the ladies from the church. They stood with Pat in a semi-circle on the front porch, and the women talked and prayed in their tribal language. It was an emotional moment at the end of the best adventure we ever had.

The Airport Scene

The airport scene when we left PNG was more poignant than the one in the movie, "Casablanca". On the day we were to leave, Rosemary spent the whole day with us. She cried at the airport and her son, Jeffrey, grieved for Ryan. Ryan consoled himself that he was going to see his grandpa, but he cried later. All of the boys from the halfway house and all of Billy's boys were at the airport to see us off. Russ told Larry to give Stephen Goilala his boots and to give Thomas the boom box.

As we inched closer to the departure gate, our friends pressed closer, and we kept stopping for last goodbyes. Pat was laden with hand made gifts, and as she greeted each of the boys one last time, she broke down in tears. She will miss each one immensely, especially her friend, the barefoot doctor.

Pat

We were changed as a result of our experiences in Papua New Guinea. We were stronger Christians, more disciplined in our devotions and freer to share our faith. From the first time I encouraged a Jesus Centre boy to not run away, I knew this was what I was supposed to be doing, and it led to all the other things I did. I never missed the "diplomatic" life, the fancy houses and air conditioning. Here in P.N.G., everything was real. We took showers in the afternoon, when the sun would warm up the water. We were with the people, helping build houses. We lived with the people and saw their strengths and weaknesses. When we needed a break, we could drive to the beautiful, mighty Sogeri Mountain. Having constant interactions with people, which at times was wearying yet rewarding, filled our days and nights.

Here I am where I ought to be. Only years later did I realize Papua New Guinea was the happiest time of my life.

After returning to the farmland and countryside of Radnor, Ohio, I would sit outside on the open front deck while the children were in their country schools. The sun would beat down, but not too hot, with the willow tree giving some shade and the swing blowing in the wind. I could see in the distance a whole train coming closer and closer. The smell of the pig farm sometimes wafted down our way. I would bring out my Bible and read and then burst into song in Pidgin, then English, with only the growing corn to hear. No matter what happened or what the future laid, I always had Papua New Guinea.

Russ

We returned to Delaware County, Ohio to a farmhouse in the middle of a cornfield. The ground was so flat you could see the whole line of a train go by. Much of the news at this time was about the civil war and starvation in Somalia. President George H.W. Bush even went to Somalia. I felt we had to get involved in the relief effort there. I contacted a number of organizations that were listed as sending relief to Somalia. Food for the Hungry International was interested in hiring me as their Somalia Country Director. They were looking for somebody with experience in Somalia, and there really weren't many of us around. The FHI project included food and seed distribution, an outpatient clinic and a mobile medical team. This was the next assignment. The family would live in Nairobi, Kenya and I would operate out of an office in Nairobi, taking trips to and from the project site in Southern Somalia. It would be a good feeling to be back in Africa, and I looked forward to my returning

95

to Somalia with trepidation because of the unknown of the conflict and chaos.

PART III
TURMOIL IN EAST AFRICA
1993 – 1995

RETURN TO SOMALIA

Russ

About 30 miles east of Nairobi, Kenya, flying at 10,000 feet, I could see the snow-capped peak of Mt. Kilimanjaro on the right and Mt. Kenya, with its broad shoulders, on the left. This was my second trip to Saakow Weyn, Somalia, but the first time the skies were clear enough to see Kilimanjaro. The relief agency for which I worked was operating a humanitarian aid project in this rural town on the Juba River about 150 miles west of Mogadishu. I was going to Saakow Weyn to appear before the town elders to discuss a security problem on the project.

Two days before, four gunmen had appeared at the gate of our outpatient clinic. They said they had occupied the building during the war, and now they wanted it back. They also said that they would be just as happy with money and jobs. Our staff members said, "no", and one of the hooligans fired a shot over the head of one of our guards. A second guard from our compound, who was from the same clan as the gunmen, told them to leave or they would have a fight on their hands. With that, the four gunmen took off and hid behind the town's old school building.

The gunmen seemed intent on hanging around and being a menace, so the U.N. troops from Bardera, a major town north of Saakow, were called in. With the arrival of the U.N. troops, the gunmen headed for the bush. The troops didn't stay long but said they would return for the bad guys if we apprehended them. Our people closed the clinic and told the local elders that it wouldn't be reopened until the troublemakers were caught and compensation paid.

Our Cessna landed on the red dirt strip outside of town just after noon. Everything seemed normal as we drove through the town. We saw a large number of people massed under the meeting tree, not far from our compound. After talking to the team leader and other field staff about the situation, we went to the tree to see the elders.

There was an unusually large turnout for the meeting. One of the old men from the west side of the Juba River spoke first and apologized for the incident. He also stated that we have a government in America, and yet the same things happen there. What should we expect in Somalia? He was right. Another one of the leaders said that he and his fellow elders appreciated our work, and didn't want anything to happen to make us leave. That, however, was about all the Somalis could concede in apologies. The next three speakers said that what's done is done. Now, they said, the important thing is that they need more donated seeds in Saakow Weyn. We had given them enough sorghum seeds, but now they needed sesame seeds, and watermelon would be nice. They also wanted us to help them get started with ground nuts again.

It was time to get back to the subject at hand. Finally it was my turn to speak. I said that we had more important things to discuss than sesame seeds and watermelon. I told them that I had been bragging about Saakow in America, and that the name "Saakow Weyn" had been spoken under a hundred shade trees in the United States. This impressed the old men, because an old Somali saying, as told to me by Hassan Hussein, is; "It's better to have your name spoken under a hundred shade trees than to own a hundred she-camels". They knew that I was indeed speaking well of their town. I told them that the recent incident was disturbing, because it was making a liar out of me.

The old boys definitely had some hometown pride. They didn't want me to be made a liar because I spoke highly of Saakow Weyn. After some more discussion and a little storytelling, the elders rededicated themselves to keeping control of troublemakers. They also agreed to pay two goats as compensation for the incident. Everyone left the meeting in a happy mood, especially one of the older men with a crooked walking stick. He was convinced that tourists from Ohio would soon be visiting Saakow.

The Civil War

Yes, I was back in Somalia, but much had changed since we were last here. The Somali National Movement (SNM), the Isaaq insurgents in the northwest, intensified its guerrilla attacks on government troops, officials and installations. In retaliation, President Siad Barre ordered the bombing of Hargeisa. The town was all but destroyed and, with reinforced troops, the government established firm control over the region. The SNM was relegated to only being able to mount harassing activities from across the Ethiopian border.

Other insurgent groups were forming in southern Somalia. In 1989 Mohamed Farah Aideed, an ex-general in Barre's army, joined the Hawiye rebels who were building up their forces in Ethiopia. This group, as well as underground groups in Mogadishu, was financed by Ali Mahdi, a prominent Abgal business man in Mogadishu. Siad Barre was tipped off to Mahdi's activities and ordered his arrest. Mahdi eluded arrest and fled north to the Mudug Region.

In late 1990 Ali Mahdi made a clandestine return to Mogadishu and assembled underground groups which he had been arming and financing.

In a series of ambushes on government troops and attacks on key government installations, Mahdi gained control of the streets of most of Mogadishu. Siad Barre and his troops were "holed-up" at the presidential palace, Villa Somalia, and losing control of the city, when Aideed and his forces arrived from Ethiopia. Aideed was keen to mount an assault on Villa Somalia and capture Barre. Mahdi wanted to talk to Barre. He thought Barre could be convinced to relinquish the presidency, and that large scale fighting in Mogadishu could be avoided.

At this point Mahdi was supported by all of the Hawiye clans in his claim to the presidency. Mahdi, however, made his first of several mistakes in the eyes of the Hawiye. He ordered the southern troops out of the northwest and back to Mogadishu. The Hawiye thought this contributed to the secession of Somaliland

Aideed and his forces were joined by other Hawiye rebels and attacked Villa Somalia, the president's home. Mahdi and the Abgal rebels sat-out this fight. Aideed chased Barre and his troops to Kismayo and returned to Mogadishu. Barre took this opportunity to regroup his troops. He moved from Kismayo to Bardera, home territory of his Marehan clan, and rebuilt his forces. He marched toward Mogadishu and advanced as far as Afgoye, 19 miles from Mogadishu.

Aideed gathered his forces for a final offensive to run Barre out of Somalia, once and for all. Mahdi still wanted to talk, but no one else was in the mood for talking. Aideed led a combined Hawiye, including Abgal, attack on Barre's position and ran the ex-president and his troops through Bardera and on into Kenya. Barre did not return to Somalia. His Marehan clan, however, waited until the Aideed forces were reduced in Bardera, and Aideed was occupied elsewhere, to return. The Marehan retook Bardera and established control as far south as the Saakow District. They relinquished control of Saakow to their fellow Darods, the Ogaden, who occupied the west side of the river in Saakow District. The balance of power would eventually change, but the Ogaden ran Saakow for some period of time. The Marehan would continue to control Bardera and the Gedo Region, and there was nothing Aideed could do about it.

Back in Mogadishu, Aideed and Mahdi were feuding. Aideed didn't think Mahdi deserved to be president, since he didn't take part in running Barre out of the country. Mahdi didn't trust Aideed, but as a result of the victory over Barre, Aideed gained support of most of the Hawiye clans. The disintegration of the Hawiye coalition resulted in inter-clan fighting in Mogadishu. The fighting intensified to the point that the historic center of Mogadishu was destroyed. Throughout the fighting to oust Siad Barre, the city's infrastructure was left intact. The Hawiye fighting was a different story. Buildings were shelled and massive looting took place.

The Hawiye gained control of Mogadishu, but immediately went about to destroy it.

The riverine regions of southern Somalia, between the Juba and Shabelli Rivers, were hardest hit by the civil war. The Rahanweyn clans which occupied this part of Somalia took a beating. They were primarily agriculturalists and not accustomed to the armed clashes that the nomadic clans so often experienced in livestock raids. As the civil war progressed, they eventually took up arms and became somewhat aligned with Aideed. The Rahanweyn started flexing their muscles, and in Saakow, this meant trouble for the Ogaden.

HORN OF THE HUNTER

Russ

I always wanted to live an African adventure like those in a Robert Ruark novel. To hunt a fine African lion with a fine English rifle would be a singular experience. The closest I had come to capturing this fantasy occurred during one of my early trips to Saakow Weyn, Somalia. I shot an antelope with an AK-47. It was quite an adventure – hunting with the Somali militia and eating wild game around a campfire. This wasn't the type of safari that novelists immortalize, but it was the nearest thing that Somalia had to offer. That was on a Wednesday. Two days later, I had a different type of experience with the clan militias of Somalia.

On that Friday morning, I was fixing my first cup of coffee when our Sudanese field officer, Cosmos Joel, came into the office and said militias were forming in the town. I looked outside, and instead of the normal flow of women and children walking toward the river, I saw groups of men walking around with guns. It was not clear what sparked this show of arms, but this was the turning point for the balance of power between the Rahanwein and the Ogadeni in the Saakow District.

Throughout the day, sporadic gunfire was heard. A war of nerves was going on between the armed populace on the west bank of the river and the town militia of Saakow Weyn on the east. Cosmos and Hung Ku Kim, our logistics officer, stayed on the radio with Swedish Church Relief on the other side of Saakow and with the UN in Bardhera. Midori Ito, our nurse, and I tried to avoid the windows. John Farmer, the team leader, and Seonaid Robertson, our medical director, were in Nairobi on rotation. There wasn't too much shooting, but every time I stuck my head out the door, I heard a bullet whistle by. As the afternoon progressed we became very worried. Large numbers of men armed with heavy, machine guns and grenades began dispersing behind our compound. These men were from distant villages to the east and came to Saakow as a show of Rahanweyn firepower. It was bad enough that locals on each side of the river were threatening each other. The fact that a large number of out-of-town gunmen were hanging around was even more troublesome. We made radio contact with the U.N. troops in Bardhera, reported that the situation in Saakow was ominous and said that we wanted to be evacuated.

As the U.N. helicopters circled Saakow Weyn, the guns disappeared from the streets. The helicopter landed at the airstrip, and Botswanan troops under U.N. command swept through Saakow Weyn on foot. More troops were arriving by road to spend the night, but passage on the road was questionable because of recent rains. It was decided that we should leave on the helicopter and return after the troops had garrisoned the town. We arrived in Bardhera fifteen minutes after the sun had set. The Russian pilot seemed to have a hard time finding the landing pad. The chopper slowed, then sped up and turned a couple of times. After landing we walked with the Botswanan troops to their headquarters, a sprawling tent city, and briefed their commander on the events in Saakow. We then got a ride to the U.N. High Commission for Refugees (UNHCR) compound to spend the night. The accommodations at the UNHCR compound looked pretty basic, but the tents were well appointed with sturdy cots. We also arrived just in time for a candlelight dinner, on a checkered tablecloth, in the mess tent. After dinner we had a warm shower and slept the night on a well made cot.

The next day I decided to find a U.N. or relief flight back to Nairobi. I missed the U.N. helicopter to Mogadishu with connecting flights to Nairobi, so I sat in the shade of another helicopter and watched the Russian crews go about their maintenance chores. I was about to doze off when, just under the brim of my cap, I spotted a blue dot gliding through the sky and heard the low purr of the engine as it descended. This was the khat flight from Nairobi. The trade in weapons and khat (a chewable leaf containing a stimulant drug) flourished as the result of fighting and turmoil in Somalia. Here was one of those ships of despair, operated by crass individuals profiteering from the war, and I was going to hitch a ride on it back to Nairobi.

These little planes, flown by mercenaries, leave Nairobi loaded with khat and usually return empty. The pilot of this one was a decent sort of fellow from South Africa. Most mercenaries in this part of the world are South Africans or refugees from the former Rhodesia. After the usual Somali haggling and chicanery, the pilot got his money. The Somalis got their khat, and I got a free ride back to Nairobi.

Peace returned to Saakow Weyn, but the balance of power had shifted. The Ogaden no longer ran the town. It was an alliance of the Rahanweyn sub-clans that would be responsible for keeping the peace.

THE BANDIT BOYS OF SAAKOW

Russ

From the veranda of the Outspan Hotel in Nyeri, Kenya, various images of Mt. Kenya are painted on the mind. As day breaks, the mountain appears as a huge shadow on the brightening horizon. In the clear, sunlit morning the snow-capped peak marks the summit of the broad mountain slopes. When the late afternoon clouds move in, they encircle the mountain, and the peak rises above the clouds to announce its majesty.

This is the scene from which I was aroused by the phone call informing me that the airplane carrying a load of cargo for various projects in our area had been attacked by bandits. The plane had been offloaded and ready for takeoff, when a young man appeared forward of the starboard engine with a grenade. The grenade was wrestled away from the man; but he grabbed an AK-47, ran to the edge of the airstrip and started shooting at the plane. Various accounts existed of the ensuing events, but the bandit and his accomplices eventually ran for the bush. One crewman had been wounded by shrapnel, and the plane sat on the airstrip disabled for two days. The U.N. troops soon arrived to evacuate the crewmen and secure the airstrip. It was a bad day for Saakow Weyn. Attempts to build a reputation as a peaceful community were shattered by the irresponsible action of a handful of local bandits.

The next couple of days were a time of uncertainty as the town elders vacillated on their response. Inter-clan conflict was apparent with the clan of the bandits taking their side. After four days of uncertainty and debate, the bandits themselves brought events to a climax on the evening after the U.N. troops had left town. They shot at one of our guards, and a gunfight flared outside of our compound. One of the bandits took a bullet to the chest, and they headed for the bush again. All the expatriates left Saakow, and relief operations were halted. Saakow Weyn acquired the nickname "Psycho Weyn".

In Saakow the clan leaders were feeling the pressure of having all relief operations shut down. Tense negotiations were taking place among the various clans. As a result of these negotiations, the bandits were turned over to the town elders by their clan. We were informed that the bandits were in custody, and that the elders had arrived at the solution to our bandit problem.

The project team leader, John Farmer, and I chartered a flight to Buaale, the town south of Saakow. We met with some of our Somali staff and then drove to Saakow for a series of meetings with the elders. The elders stated that bandits would not be tolerated no matter what clan, and that they could be shot without repercussions to those doing the shooting. The "final solution" for the bandits in custody was that they would take an oath on the Koran that they would never again threaten or shoot at us. At first glance, this did not seem to be a good solution to our problem. However, after discussing the proposal with our Somali staff, it was accepted that the oath was the best thing to do. There was no law or justice system in Somalia. The payment of compensation didn't work. A bandit could shoot at you one day, pay a goat as compensation and then shoot at you again the next day. The oath was a deterrent, because the consequence of not keeping the oath was death, and the sentence could not be commuted.

The next day dawned as usual with the soothing night breeze giving way to the harsh Somali sun. Our second meeting with the elders convened, but tension gripped the air. Certain elders brought up old questions and wanted to discuss the reason for the bandits' actions. We said that their reasons were no longer of concern, and that they did more harm to the community by their actions than any perceived harm that could have been done to them. After a bit of debate about the purpose of the meeting, the bandits were brought forward. The Koran was placed before them, and we were ready for the ceremony. But first, the boys had a prepared statement that they wanted me to read. I refused to take the statement and reiterated that we were meeting to settle matters and not debate old issues. The boys acted like they wanted to run the meeting rather than presenting themselves in a contrite manner. One boy started to walk out. Somebody called him back. Two elders jumped up and said that taking the oath was a dangerous thing to do and ushered the boys out of the meeting. With that, the other elders jumped up and pointed their fingers at the elders who were siding with the boys and said, "Now it is clear who the troublemakers are and why these bandits can't be controlled". We left the meeting with everyone shouting at each other and breaking off into small groups.

It looked as though we were back to square one with maybe even a tribal war in the offing. About an hour after the meeting, three leaders of one of the local clans stopped by our office to talk. They said that their clan was the strongest in town, and they wanted to assure us that we were under their protection. This was somewhat reassuring but still not conducive to a good night's sleep.

The elders must have done a lot of talking and arm-twisting that night. The next day we had our third meeting under the shade of the same, old meeting tree. Peace was in the air. The elders asked if we were ready to receive the boys and take their oath. We said, "Sure". The bandit boys appeared before us and all of the leadership of Saakow District. They took their oath. We shook their hands and stated that the old is finished, and it's a new day for Saakow. This time the boys seemed repentant and happy to have the whole thing over. We slept well that night, and the next day dawned with new hope for Saakow.

Donkey Cart in Saakow Weyn, Somalia

Project Office Saakow Weyn, Somalia

View from inside the old Bank building, Saakow Weyn, Somalia

Project Guards, Saakow Weyn, Somalia

Project Guards on the Juba River

PAT'S RETURN TO SOMALIA

Pat

The light plane swept over the red dirt airstrip once. The gray-haired pilot turned his head toward me and smiled. I asked, "That's it?" He nodded, turned the plane and banked it for the approach. After five long years I was returning to Somalia – not to Mogadishu, the capital, but to Saakow Weyn, a small, rural village. I put on one of my Somali shawls I had collected beforehand to cover my head. This was rural, traditional Somalia, not the urban center that Mogadishu once was.

The warm, humid air was a welcome relief from the confines of the Cessna 404. I tried to overlook the loaded AK-47s that our project guards were holding as I greeted them. Their smiles were warm, and their handshakes warmed my fingers, chilled during the two and a half hour flight from Nairobi. I always thought that I would kiss the ground if I ever came back to Somalia, but I only knelt and patted the red soil. Two young Somali boys in the distance were leaning on a reed with one leg poised against the other. I motioned for them to come closer, but they stood still. I raised my hand to show them that I had something, and I walked toward them. They slowly came forward to me. I gave each of them a lollipop, and they smiled. As I left, I saw them in the same position as before, except that each had a small, white lollipop stick protruding from his mouth.

An old, army-green Land Rover truck was waiting to take us and the relief supplies into town. The guards sat in the truck bed holding onto their rifles. The red dirt turned to white sand and scrub bushes on the short drive to town. Inside the compound was a huge tent used to store grain and relief supplies. It dwarfed the staff house and clinic. The tent was now empty of its contents and its controversy. When it was full of food, a major build up of armed militia occurred in town. Looting seemed possible with such a large quantity of food as a target, so a hasty distribution of grain was made to the local farmers.

We ate lunch right away. One of the Somali staff was going to get married, and Russ said it would be more prosperous to buy camels than to buy a wife. The Somalis said, "Yes, but camels don't produce children!" We all laughed and washed down the spaghetti and fresh tomatoes and onions with cans of Coke. The local sambusas, a crunchy shell stuffed with spicy, camel meat, were especially good. I ate five, one after the other, until the Somalis offered for me to take the other twenty home.

I was anxious to see Saakow Weyn. Although the population of the town was estimated at 5,000, it seemed much smaller. We passed the famous meeting tree where town elders conducted important meetings and made decisions. Its long branches covered a large area, including a seating area of cement blocks similar to an amphitheater. We passed by a donkey in an abandoned building, the local bank. One after the other, broken-down buildings that once were part of local life stood helpless under the Somali sun: the women's building, the police station and the school. There was life in coming out of the mosque, the only building that had been rebuilt. As I walked through the marketplace with our guards, I saw a young boy with a rifle. He was part of the militia. Sometimes many militiamen were in the streets and sometimes none. Today there was this one boy. He smiled for the camera, and I saw that his front teeth were missing. None of the townspeople came up to us, and I only talked briefly to a couple of the elders. My eye caught sight of a bright red and blue Somali shawl. I got the price down to ten dollars and took home a colorful Somali shawl. Deep into the market I discovered frankincense and other exotic herbs. I bought a handful of frankincense, and the seller wadded it up in a piece of paper for me to take home.

Instead of watching for cars in the street, we had to make way for donkey carts. Young boys drove the carts, carrying water or commodities to and from the river or the market. I heard the sing-song voices of children. We passed an open "school" where six children were sitting on the ground with Koran boards. They used the wood boards to write verses from the Koran with a reed and homemade ink. The children stopped for me to take a photo. Agreeing to be photographed was unheard of in pre-war Somalia, especially in a Koranic school.

The Juba River was close to our compound. People fetched water from the river and the women washed clothes in the river. The river flooded during the rainy season, and as the water receded, the Somalis planted maize and vegetables in the flood plains. The river was also the boundary between two clan groups, the nomadic Ogaden on the west side and the more settled, agricultural Rahanweyn on the east. When clan tensions rose, neither side crossed the river. Although there was no open hostility on this day, the Ogaden were not allowed to cross the river because of a recent shooting incident. Crocodiles were a constant danger near the river. In fact, I saw a man who had been badly bitten by a croc. He was lying on a mat on the ground at the clinic. His hands and feet were bandaged, but he was alive.

As the hours passed, it was getting uncomfortably warm. My head covering kept slipping off, and I was impatiently rearranging it. I asked for some Somalia tea, a deliciously sweet drink with aromatic spices, so we returned to the compound and drank tea on the flat roof of the veranda. This second storey sitting area was shaded with locally made mats, and a breeze brought quick relief from the heat. Abdurahman, the Somali field officer who spoke excellent English, was sitting with me. I showed him a couple of Christian comic books that were translated into the Somali language. Having this type of material was generally dangerous for a Somali, but during this point in the civil war, such issues weren't as significant. They had clans, militia and thieves to worry about, so Christian proselytizing wasn't utmost in their minds.

Outside the compound, the green truck was waiting to take us back to the airplane. One of the guards said, "You see the buildings. They are broken down, like the people here are broken down." Another guard continued, "They are fighting over a piece of paper. The chairman of the elders committee says that only he can sign a paper coming from the committee. He threatened to have his hands cut off, if anyone else adds their name." It was frustrating even for these Somalis. I said, "They must think about their children and their children's children. They need to tear down these old, broken down buildings and begin building new ones."

Peace in Somalia seemed so elusive but not impossible. If the people had one goal to work toward, they could overlook their differences. We had to leave. The pilot had been waiting with the plane for three hours. As we piled into the truck, I had a better sense of Saakow Weyn. I was even comfortable with the guns. At the airstrip we shook hands all around, and I passed out more lollipops. I handed the bag of remaining lollipops to one of the guards. As Russ and I climbed into the plane, I immediately removed my shawl. As we were waving our last farewells, I saw the guard with the bag of lollipops put it behind his back, as if he and the others were fighting over the candy. Somehow I still loved this land and the people, but I wasn't ready to make my home here again.

SHABA SAFARI

Russ

The lush, green hills of the Aberdare Mountain Range were a stark contrast to the arid land of southern Somalia, home of our Somali companions. Several miles north of Nanyuki, Kenya, however, we got our first view of the vast expanse of the arid Samburu country. With the foothills of Mt. Kenya to our backs, we descended into the ochre plains dotted with volcanic monoliths. At the end of the descent was the town of Isiolo. With its mixture of Samburu, Somali, Boran and Turkana populations; Isiolo was the gateway to Kenya's Northern Frontier District. We were having a staff retreat that included the expatriates, our Kenyan staff from the Nairobi office and key Somali staff from Saakow Weyn. We were on our way to Shaba National Reserve, one of Kenya's newest parks and home of the reticulated giraffe and other rare game species unique to this part of Kenya.

Archer's Post, a few miles beyond Isiolo, appeared to be no more than a gate and the point where the tarmac ended. Driving the dusty, dirt road from Archer's Post to the park entrance, we wondered what animal other than a camel or dik-dik could survive in this barren land. Thanks to the Uaso Nyiro River, with its palm-fringed banks cutting through this semi-desert country, a wide variety of game made their homes in Shaba and the neighboring Samburu and Buffalo Springs Reserves. The reticulated giraffe as well as Grevy's zebra, Beisa Oryx, the long-necked gerenuk and the Somali ostrich were the wildlife unique to this area. The elephants of the Uaso Nyiro roamed the numerous dry washes leading from the river and were easily seen in small herds feeding along the river bank.

One of the premier, but lesser known, resorts of Kenya was the Sarova Shaba. Set as an oasis on the Uaso Nyiro River, spring water was channeled through the grounds of the lodge as a stark contrast to the arid surroundings. The lodge facilities had an open-air restaurant, and the guest quarters were appropriately designed with thatch roofs and built of local mazera stone and timber. A Samburu tribesman stood guard in the dining area to chase away the pesky vervet monkeys, ravens and weavers. After dinner the guests were entertained by Samburu dancers. The young warriors, who were related to the Masaii and dressed similarly with red togas, jumped high in the air with knees locked and uttered guttural grunts. The women shook their mass of neck beads by thrusting their neck and shoulders backward and forward. One girl shrieked a volley of vowel sounds, and then one of the men grunted and jumped in the air again. The guy who jumped the highest got the girl.

One of the most "guest friendly" practices of Kenya's resorts was full board accommodation. Included with lodging was a full buffet and order grill at each meal. The food was good and plentiful with any buffet item expected for breakfast, lunch and dinner and several meat choices from the grill. From Mombasa to Lake Turkana the traveler can eat well if staying at Kenya's resort hotels. Americans are unaccustomed to the British tradition of serving coffee after, rather than with, the dessert. At various times and in various parts of the Commonwealth, I poured my own coffee from the waiter's station, because the staff was trained not to serve coffee until after the dessert.

The more mature, neighboring game reserves of Samburu and Buffalo Springs offered public camp sites and lodges with tented camps. The oldest of the game lodges in the area was the Samburu Game Lodge which was also situated on the Uaso Nyiro River. The lodge was a traditional, stone structure with a "Makati" (timber and thatch) roof. Guest accommodations consisted of self contained cottages strung out along the river. Evening entertainment at the Samburu Game Lodge included Samburu dancers and viewing a baited tree along the river in hope of seeing a leopard. The wait was worthwhile when a "Greta Garbo" of the animal kingdom made an appearance. The Samburu country was not as popular with tourists as some of Kenya's other resort areas such as Masaii Mara or Amboselli. This was good, because it wasn't necessary to fight for position with other tour vans and Land Rovers at a lion kill.

After several years of living in East Africa, I eventually realized the importance of camera equipment and knowledge of photography in making the most of game viewing trips. The pursuit of that definitive photo of the beast of your choice was a challenging venture and could be habit-forming. The visitor to Africa's game parks, who hadn't taken photography seriously in the past, would greatly appreciate a good camera and knowing how to use it. The reticulated giraffe often posed for a picture, but the Beisa Oryx was a shy animal and required much patience and the right equipment to get that definitive shot. The old "white hunters" of colonial times in Africa were certain to be armed with their Holland and Holland double rifle not the barnyard plinking gun. Similarly for today's tourists and their camera equipment, what's good for the family picnic may fall short on a game-drive.

It was interesting to see everyone's reaction to our oasis in the desert. My wife said that the best part of her day was walking out of the Banda in the morning to a quietness accented by the clean, bright morning sun.

Abdurahman and Ahmed, having just arrived from Saakow Weyn, Somalia, thought they had died and gone to heaven. We weren't sure whose heaven, since they were Muslim and the rest of us were Christian and the organization was Christian. We had meetings about relief work and the vision of the organization. As part of these meetings we had devotions, and discussions about Christianity. Abdurahman and Ahmed, our lead Somali staff in Saakow, skipped out of this part of the meetings. Ahmed said, "I'm going to go talk to Pat." Pat was waiting, and she continued the discussions about God and Jesus. This was like jumping out of the frying pan and into the fire for Ahmed. Ahmed seemed extremely paranoid about religious matters. In fact one time when we were taking group photos and everybody said, "cheese", Ahmed ran off. He thought we said, "Jesus".

Sarah Waitindi, our Kenyan accountant, kept the waiters in line to make sure that they didn't overcharge for drinks, and she seemed to enjoy negotiating room upgrades with the Kikuyu manager. Our Kenyan staff enjoyed the game drives more than I expected. Kenyans seem to have a blasé attitude about African wildlife, but our group was up at 5:00 for our early morning photos safaris.

Our first morning of game viewing was the most successful. A herd of Grevy's zebra crossed the road directly ahead of us. I read that Grevy's zebras didn't congregate in herds like the common zebra, but we saw several large herds of Grevy's on this trip. The Beisa Oryx seemed shy, and as we approached distant herds, they drifted away from our approaching vehicle. A close look into the thick bush usually revealed a long-necked gerenuk stretching to reach the green leaves of a thorn bush. This country was arid and sparse in some areas, but the game reserves bordering the Uaso Nyiro River had a considerable amount of cover, and the terrain was rolling rather than flat.

As we crested a hill after failing to get close to a large herd of Oryx, we were met by several reticulated giraffe on each side of the road. These animals weren't shy but went about their browsing and stopped to pose for our cameras between bites.

Several months after the trip, I asked Ryan, who was 8 years old at the time, what he remembered most. He said, "Mommy going to the bathroom and the elephant". Our second game drive started slowly. We drove around a hill several times looking for a pride of lions but couldn't find them. My wife and several others of the party had to relieve their bladders, so we asked the drivers of the two vans to find a nice, safe area with plenty of trees. Those who had to pee scrambled around looking for a good tree. Those left in the vans laughed and said beware of chui (Swahili for leopard).

After the rest stop we followed a trail along the river and spotted a small herd of elephants on the on the far side. As we proceeded along a dirt road and around a bend, we spotted a lone bull elephant among some trees on a hillside. Our two vans drove up a path toward the elephant, with my van in the rear. The elephant at first seemed curious about the lead van and slowly walked toward it with his trunk in the air but not trumpeting. He then seemed irritated, spread his ears, bellowed and charged the van. From the perspective of those in the lead van, he not only dwarfed the van, but was so close as to be a blur of gray in their camera lenses. The lead driver seemed to have a hard time finding reverse, but after backing the van off a bit, the elephant half circled and stood still to watch us retreat.

The game drives were the primary reason to take a safari, but the kids also enjoyed the swimming pool, watching the Samburu dancers and feeding the crocodiles that visited the river bank at night. The adults enjoyed the times of relaxation and eating between game drives and meetings. For those of our party who had been on many safaris in East Africa, as well as those who hadn't, the Shaba safari along the Uaso Nyiro River was a unique experience.

Reticulated Giraffe in Shaba and Buffalo Springs Game Reserve

Grevy's Zebra Shaba and Buffalo Springs Game Reserve

Samburu and the tourist Near Wamba, Kenya

Outspan Hotel Nyeri, Kenya

Lake Naivasha: Laura, Pat, Ryan, Katie and guide

Sarova Shaba Pool

RWANDAN REFUGEE CRISIS

Russ

The work in Somalia was settling down to a routine, and the security situation in Saakow District became stable. The humanitarian crisis in Somalia was ebbing and on its heels came the Rwanda blood bath. I was asked to go to a place called Ngara, Tanzania, where Rwandan refugees were pouring across the border at an unprecedented rate. The purpose of the trip was to see if there was anything our organization could do. I radioed Saakow and asked our Medical Coordinator, Seonaid Robertson to pack her bags. I asked Emmanuel Habiyambere, our Tutsi administrative assistant in Nairobi, if he wanted to see Rwanda. He said, "Sure". Emmanuel fled Rwanda with his family in 1960 during that Hutu uprising, and he hadn't seen Rwanda since. We booked a flight to Mwanza, Tanzania, and from there hired a Land Rover for the two day drive over rough, washed-out roads to Ngara.

Ngara was literally at the end of the road. Just across the Kagera River, however, lied war ravaged Rwanda, and over the hill from Ngara was the largest refugee camp in the world. In this rugged part of Tanzania, west of Lake Victoria, more than 300,000 Rwandan refugees were encamped, and 250,000 of them of them were in the Benaco Camp near Ngara. At river crossings along the Kagera and through the swamp at Kaisho, thousands of fleeing Rwandans entered Tanzania each day.

After the destruction of the airplane carrying the presidents of Rwanda and Burundi, rebels of the Rwanda Patriotic Front (RPF) swept through the Kagera National Park and on to besiege Kigale, the capital of Rwanda. In front of the Tutsi-dominated RPF, fanatics of the rival Hutus killed hundreds of thousands of innocent civilians, Tutsi and Hutu alike. The death toll in one month rivaled that of the Vietnam War. As the rebels advanced toward the Rusomo Bridge, a major border crossing, the Rwandan government soldiers abandoned their posts and escaped into Tanzania. These men had been killing civilians, and now they were hiding in the refugee camps. Emmanuel and I heard about some Rwandan soldiers who were brought to the Murgwanza Hospital in Ngara. They exposed who they were by bragging about having slain Tutsis. We went over to the hospital to interview these characters, but the Tanzanian Army had carried them off to jail in the middle of the night.

After the Rwandan troops abandoned the Rusomo Bridge, thousands of Rwandans swarmed across it. The Tanzanian authorities did not try to stop them. Tanzania had historically been open to refugees from conflicts and natural disasters in Central Africa. This is proper since much of Tanzania's vast countryside is sparsely populated, while Rwanda, Burundi and other nations bordering Tanzania are among the most densely populated in the world.

Ngara was not only invaded by hordes of refugees but also by hordes of relief agencies with trucks, Land Rovers and money to spend. The missionaries at the Murgwanza Hospital called it the "NGO Wars". "NGO" is the acronym for nongovernmental organization which is another term for relief agency. They all arrived at Ngara and were vying for a piece of the action. The U.N. had selected certain NGOs to work in the refugee camps, and the others played the role of understudies looking for a niche to fill. It was important to act quickly and not be left in the dust by those who arrived before us. Many refugees were crossing into Tanzania farther north along the Rwanda border and in a loop even further north through Uganda. The area north had fewer NGOs, so that's where we headed. At Kigarema a makeshift refugee camp was growing by the hour. The road on north to Kaisho was a procession of refugees in scattered groups of 10 to 30. The hospital at Kaisho was stretched to its limit by refugees in need of medical attention, and it had few resources. We made arrangements to supply the hospital with medicine and provide some temporary nursing help.

The trip was bittersweet for Emmanuel. He was able to view the green hills of Rwanda for the first time in thirty years, but he was also reminded of his displacement and wandering as a refugee those many years ago. In Kaisho he visited an aunt whom he hadn't seen for many years. She was one of the many Tutsis who fled Rwanda in the 1960s and settled in villages along the border in Tanzania or Uganda. It was from this Diaspora that emerged the sons who built the RPF.

We returned to Mwanza by a ferry from Bukoba, a port on the western shores of Lake Victoria. Seonaid and Emmanuel were remaining in Mwanza to accompany some colleagues from another relief agency to Ngara, and I was returning to Nairobi by way of Dar Es Salam to make arrangements for more assistance to the hospital at Kaisho. As I was waiting in the Mwanza airport for my flight to Dar, a huge shadow passed over the terminal. A USAF C-5 cargo plane was landing with massive amounts of supplies and equipment for the relief effort. I discovered that watching these huge planes come and go was a major spectator event in Mwanza. This was the largest refugee movement since World War II. The response to it was massive and the impact on the towns and villages in western Tanzania was overwhelming. The Rwanda refugee crisis was not over, however, and there were other towns in other places that were even more disrupted than Mwanza, Ngara and the villages along the Kagera River. What will I see next on the border of Rwanda?

Rusumo Bridge from Rwanda to Tanzania

Rusumo, Tanzania Red Cross Station

HELL IN GOMA

Russ

"There is a great chasm separating us and anyone wanting to come to you from here is stopped at the edge. And no one over there can cross to us." This is how the Bible describes the gap between Paradise and Hades. Driving past the Rwandan refugee camps scattered to the north and west of Goma, Zaire was like gazing into hell. The moonscape of lava rock and black grit with a constant haze of smoke and dust looked like hell. The litter of the refugee population was oral rehydration bags and dead bodies. The place smelled like hell.

When Rwandan refugees started moving westward into Zaire, the situation was far worse than that in Tanzania. The refugees coming into Zaire were dying like flies from cholera. I went to Goma to prepare the way for our Somalia team to set up a relief operation in response to this disaster. In Nairobi I loaded our old pick-up truck and a supply of medicine onto a C-130 for transit to Goma. I hired two Kenyan nurses, Dorcas and Edwina, who had experience with relief operations. They could help set something up. Regardless of what we found upon our arrival in Goma, I wanted to be ready to do something other than look around. We then booked an Air Zaire flight to Goma which was supposed to arrive on the tail of the C-130 carrying our truck and supplies.

On the flight to Goma we met Dr. Willy, a Zairian doctor, who, in the short term, would prove to be a great help to us in Goma. I also talked to a student who was among a group of well-heeled Rwandan refugees who had flown to Nairobi but were turned back by Kenyan immigration authorities. His father, a judge, had been killed by the Hutu militia. The rest of the family left Rwanda out of fear of the Tutsi rebel forces, the RPF. It seemed that Rwandans had to be partisans of either the RPF or the militant Hutus. Otherwise, those in the middle were in danger of being killed by either side.

The C-130 made it to Goma on time, but our Air Zaire flight was delayed by an unscheduled stop for the night in Kisangani, Zaire. The only activity at the Kisangani airport was by French troops who had set up a support base for their operations into Rwanda. We would have been in bad shape if not for the troops who opened the bar and served combat rations to the stranded passengers. We sang "Les Marseilles" just like in my favorite movie, "Casablanca", and we had a better time here than we were going to have in Goma. Two American college students were on the flight, and they kept saying, "Wow, this is surreal". I asked them what organization they were with and what they were going to do in Goma. They said they were going to "see the gorillas". If they thought the stop in Kisangani was surreal, I couldn't imagine what these two, young tourists were going to think about the unreal death and misery that remained to be seen in Goma.

The airport at Goma, bustling with military and media encampments, had relief flights landing and taking off every ten minutes. The road from the airport to town was clogged with wandering and encamped refugees. Each morning trucks picked up corpses along the roadside. The streets were littered with the diseased, meager personal effects of the dead. As bad as the scene was in Goma, it was tame preparation for what lied ahead on the road through the refugee camps. The stench of death, like everything rotten and stale that can be imagined, pervaded Goma but was magnified near the camps where wrapped bodies lined the road by the hundreds.

While passing one camp; Dorcas, Edwina and Dr. Willy wanted to get out and walk up to the Red Cross tent. I noticed the dead bodies and the filth between the road and the tent, so I said, "I'll guard the truck". From where I was parked, the body of a dead man, with his mouth open from his last gasp of air, was on my immediate left. On my right, a woman and two small children sat cooking beans in a small pot next to another corpse. This one was partially wrapped in cloth, but one arm was sticking up in the air. These refugees were all Hutus. They were running away from Tutsis but ran straight into the shadow of death.

The Zairians in and around Goma were, generally, Hutu partisans. Many anti-Tutsi rumors circulated in the town. Some refugees were said to have attempted to return to Rwanda but came back to Goma with hands cut off and other stories of mistreatment by the RPF. It was rumored that Hutus were dying from a mysterious Tutsi poison. The poison was a powder and would either be placed in food destined for Hutus or could be passed through a handshake. The recipient of the handshake, preferably a Hutu militiaman, would die after touching his lips with his hand.

The magnitude of the refugee crisis in Goma was far beyond anything that any of us could have imagined. The amount of medical supplies that we brought was insignificant compared to the extent of the need. With the chaos in the town and in the camps and the way that relief agencies were overwhelmed, we felt fortunate that we were able to set up temporary accommodations and an office. It was with great joy that I met John, Seonaid, Cosmos, Kim and Midori – the Somalia team – at the Goma airport. They stayed to work in Goma, and I was able to return to the tranquility of Saakow Weyn, Somalia.

SUMMIT MEETING IN LIBOI

Russ

Saakow Weyn quickly recovered from the war with the help of the relief agencies in the area: Food for the Hungry, Swedish Church Relief and International Rescue Committee. The U.N. High Commission for Refugees coordinated the relief activities in the Juba Valley and financed many of our projects. The town south of Saakow, Buaale, which was a commercial hub before the war, didn't recover as well as Saakow. Relief and U.N. agencies came and went, and since the meetings in Liboi, Kenya, none had returned.

Liboi was a hot, dusty town on the Somali border. The geography and the people were Somali, and many refugees from the civil war in Somalia were living in camps in Liboi and nearby Dadab. These were not squalid camps like those housing Rwandan refugees in Goma, Zaire. They were bustling communities, whose prosperity was fueled by goods looted in Somalia and later sold in Kenya. This was Kenya's Northern Frontier District, where Kenyan authorities had little control. Here, camel rustling and armed banditry were almost as bad as in Somalia.

Representatives of the U.N. High Commission for Refugees had invited me and several relief agencies to meet in Liboi with the elders from Buaale. Buaale had grown quickly from a ghost town to a wild, frontier-type community with many bandits and misfits. The town was politically unstable, and security was always a problem for relief agencies working there. Various armed militia groups attempted to extort landing fees for the use of the Buaale airstrip. Many attempts were made to hijack vehicles and relief supplies. Late one night a grenade was thrown into the UNHCR compound, but nobody was hurt.

All this criminal activity came to a climax one morning, when a Swiss journalist was killed in a hail of bullets while sitting outside of a tea shop. The murder resulted in the evacuation of all expatriates from Buaale, and a joint prohibition from the UNHCR and relief agency headquarters of any further activity or expatriate presence in the town.

We convened the Liboi meeting with the Buaale elders. We wanted to learn the motive behind the journalist's murder, to present the conditions under which relief agencies would return to Buaale, and to try to determine if the agencies' assets in the town were more likely to be looted or safeguarded while all the expatriates were gone.

Initially the murder was said to have been the work of Islamic fundamentalists, who had a training camp in Somalia near the Kenyan border. In the meeting, however, the elders claimed that the camp was actually operated by the warlord, Omar Jess, and that the killers were not necessarily Islamic fundamentalists. If the killers were not fundamentalists, then the theory was that the sub-clan in Afmadow (Mohamed Subir) was jealous of the sub-clan in Buaale (mostly Aulihan). The motive behind the murder was never certain. We determined that relief supplies and equipment left in Buaale would be safeguarded by the elders in the hope of the relief workers returning. Our discussions about a safe environment in which to work and actions expected by the community leaders resulted in many commitments and promises by the elders.

We knew, however, that keeping promises was not a Somali trait, and that Somalis elders could be fickle. This was evidenced in the last half hour of our meetings. Despite three days of conciliatory talks, a heated argument broke out between Roland Henryson, the UNHCR Buaale Team Leader, and three of the elders about payment of salaries for the airstrip security guards. Someone called the elders a bunch of thieves, and the elders suggested that the U.N. didn't really want to return to Buaale. The meeting broke up without the planned picture taking ceremony, and the Somalis returned home across the border.

We hopped into our truck and headed back to the U.N. compound in Dadab. On the road we discussed the wildlife of the area and how much more entertaining it was to be cruising in the Northern Frontier District than to be in our offices back in Nairobi. Maybe we didn't want to return to Buaale after all. I actually thought "piss on these Ogaden guys", but it was fun staying in the UNHCR tents for a couple of nights and eating UNHCR food. The other guys in the truck were probably thinking the same thing.

FOOD AND GUNS IN SAAKOW

Russ

Sambusas (a crispy sorghum flour shell stuffed with minced camel meat) from Saakow Weyn were the world's best. Our menu in Saakow was pretty much the same from day to day, but what we had was good. The bread for breakfast was baked that morning in brick ovens. Lunch was usually spaghetti and tomato sauce with fresh goat meat. The evening meals were the most varied. Someone would occasionally catch a catfish in the Juba River, or if we went hunting, we usually brought back dik-dik or guinea fowl. Regardless of the "catch of the day", it was always cooked the same way-simmered in a big pot of oil. Habibe was a young Adjuran girl and one of our first employees in Saakow. She did most of the cooking and cleaning as well as buying sambusas and provisions in town. For fish and game, however, Kasam, our ever-present casual laborer and jack-of-all-trades, did the food preparation. He would clean and dress the game, then boil it in oil outside in a little shed where they prepared food. The guards and I would sit around in the compound chewing on bones and swapping stories about Mogadishu before the war.

My observation of the guards and how they handled their rifles during our hunting expeditions confirmed the general impression that those from the sedentary clans were less proficient with firearms than those from the nomadic clans. Mahdi Mohamed, our chief of security, and some of our best guards, like Aden Buralle, were former soldiers and knew how to shoot; they were mostly from nomadic clans.

Our best rifleman was Hersi Rhoble. He was with Aideed in Ethiopia as early as 1989. His Habar Gidir clan had actually been fighting Siad Barre's Marehan clan for centuries. Marehan control of Bardhera on the Juba River was a result of land-grabbing by the Barre government. Their original home territory was centered on Dhusa Marehb, in central Somalia and bordering Habar Gidir territory. It was said that the Marehan and Habar Gidir haven't had two consecutive days of peace in two hundred years.

When the bandit boys tried to cause trouble after the U.N. troops left, it was Hersi they picked on. That was their fatal mistake. Hersi was walking to town that evening, and the bandit boys were hiding behind a building close to our compound. They grabbed Hersi and were going to take him hostage. Hersi knocked one of the boys down and broke loose.

He ran to a tree before the bandits gained their composure and started shooting.

Hersi ducked and weaved, dodging bullets, and made it to the compound. He grabbed his gun and said, "I know how to handle those kinds of characters." He and the other riflemen of our guard force, led by Mahdi Mohamed, made a military-style assault on the bandit boys' position. The boys quickly ran off into the bush with one of them carrying a bullet in his rib cage.

Another guard who knew how to handle a rifle was Ramadan Sheikh. He was Malimweyn, which was a sub-clan of the Rahanweyn, but they did a lot of camel herding, and their land bordered the Bardera Marehan. The common denominators for a tradition of handling firearms seemed to be camel herding and living next to the Marehan. The time the cargo plane was attacked by bandits at the airstrip, it was Ramadan who wrestled the grenade away from the guy who started the trouble. This was before he was one of our guards, and that was the reason we hired him. Ramadan had an interesting perspective of the clans. He said that Darod and Hawiye filled Somalia, but Dir filled the world. This may be true since other pastoral tribes in Africa have a link to Somalis.

Our guards from the predominately agricultural clans were a different story. I watched two of them shoot at a dik-dik once, and they didn't know how to hold a rifle. In America, every farmer knows how to shoot a gun. It really surprised me that these Somali farm boys aimed a rifle like an old woman would point a broom at a peddler. Also in thinking back on some of our brushes with bandits, the Rahanweyn generally were the ones ducking rather than shooting. On one hand this was smart. On the other hand, they presented themselves as hired guns for the job and should have been ready to accept the consequences. Much of our hiring, however, was political. We had to hire a mix of people from the various sub clans.

It was good to have guards who knew how to shoot. For the rest of the country, I didn't know if it was worse to have a bunch of people who couldn't shoot straight running around with guns, or those who had a deadly aim.

Summit Meeting in Liboi
Roland Henryson and Ogadeni elders

UNHCR Camp in Dadab, Kenya

GUESS WHO'S COMING ON SAFARI

Russ

People from all the tribes of East Africa as well as the turbaned Sikhs and the truculent Somalis passed by on the streets of Nairobi. The Somalis of Nairobi were often the scapegoats for many of Nairobi's social and crime problems, and they shoulder more than their share of the blame for such problems. Kenyans remembered the Shifta Wars of the 1960s when Somali bandits terrorized the Northern Frontier District. This undercurrent of animosity that Kenyans had for Somalis made it a struggle when I decided to bring seven Somali leaders of the Saakow District into Kenya for a meeting.

The Saakow elders had been complaining about our hiring practices and weren't cooperating in the community based rehabilitation projects that were replacing the relief hand-outs. I determined that a meeting in Kenya was necessary at this important juncture in the rehabilitation work. I thought it would be good to isolate the elders from their local peer pressure and to build a consensus on how to share responsibility for development work in the district. It was also a good opportunity to publicize the relative stability and peace of Saakow in contrast to the turmoil in other parts of Somalia.

After a month of haggling with the Kenyan immigration authorities to approve the trip, the Somalis arrived at Wilson airport in Nairobi. The participants included five elders. (Ugas means King):

1. Abdi Dubai, Ugas of the Geledle clan
2. Maday Malak, Ugas of the Malimweyn clan
3. Gedo Mohamed Balash, Ugas of the Leysan clan
4. Mohamed Aden, chief elder of the Hawadle clan in Saakow District
5. Aden Moktar, Ugas of the Yantar clan.

Abdurahman Mohamed, our field officer, and Mahdi Mohamed, our chief of security, attended as representatives of the Somali staff in Saakow. This was the first time for any of these men to visit Nairobi, except for Abdurahman, who attended our staff retreat with Ahmed Omar the previous year.

The exposure to a modern city such as Nairobi and the relatively developed infrastructure of the rural areas was a source of inspiration in the elders' desire to see their community rebuilt. I also saw the elders in a new light on this trip. In the past, during times of conflict, I viewed them as volatile enemies held together in a tenuous truce. As I got to know them better and watched them interact on a personal level, I realized that these guys were like childhood friends, but had developed an intense rivalry between each other.

This rivalry was exacerbated by their positions of clan leadership and the pressures of their responsibility to the clan. At our first dinner together in Nairobi, Abdi Dubai and Gedo Mohamed squabbled like my kids did at the dinner table. Gedo was talking about the time I visited his village and had a goat feast. Abdi Dubai said I shouldn't have anymore goat feasts at Gedo's village, until I visited his village. Maday Malak chimed in that my next goat feast would be at one of his villages. Such mundane squabbles even sounded worse, because of the way Somalis talked. A normal conversation sounded like an argument. When they got excited, their voices rose and the bystander was certain that a fight would erupt.

Maralal, an isolated town in the arid Samburu country of Kenya, was chosen as the location for our meetings because of its isolation from outside influences or disruptions. Our meetings were successful in reaching agreements on detailed plans for development work in the Saakow District. We weren't quite as isolated from outside Somali influences as I had anticipated. Several members of our delegation made contacts in Maralal town and supplied themselves with several bundles of khat.

The climax of the trip to Kenya was a press conference in Nairobi. The elders publicized to the assembled press corps, representing the Kenyan news media and several international news organizations, the stability of the Saakow District and their desire to see more development activity in the district. It seemed like the reporters were anxious to hear what they said.

The Somalis also took some verbal punches at UNOSOM (United Nations Operation in Somalia). Ugas Gedo Mohamed said, "UNOSOM has wasted money, and development work will proceed more smoothly once UNOSOM leaves Somalia." The UNOSOM bashing by the Somalis was not surprising. What was noteworthy was that many of UNOSOM's sister U.N. agencies, such as UNDP (United Nations Development Program) and UNICEF (United Nations International Children Education Fund) had voiced the same sentiments as that of the Somalis.

The elders also discussed the political structure and leadership of the Saakow District which contributed to its stability. Most of the people of the district relied upon their farms for their livelihood. With the help of relief organizations they rebuilt their farms and had an investment in the land. Their challenge to the rest of Somalia was "go back to work". The elders of Saakow Weyn were not unlike the leaders of other parts of Somalia in that they always wanted more, but in the case of the Saakow elders, they wanted more development for their community not just more power for themselves.

The Saakow community was excited about their leaders' visit to Kenya and the publicity that resulted for the town. I also saw a new attitude about community work and cooperation as well as increased attempts to convince me to accept a piece of farmland on the Juba River, as well as a Somali wife. Best of all, on my next visit to Saakow, I had many goat feasts to attend.

STREET CHILDREN IN NAIROBI, KENYA

Pat

When Russ returned from one of his trips to Somalia, the first thing I told him was, "I did it." He asked, "Did what?" "I started feeding the street kids!" I replied excitedly.

The first time through Nairobi, on our way to Mogadishu, Somalia, my mind was on what lay before me in Mogadishu. I barely paid attention to the children rummaging through the overflowing garbage dumpsters, with spoilage spilling out like leaves falling from a tree. I gave the situation no further thought. However, in October of 1993 when we returned to Nairobi to live, street urchins were everywhere. Nairobi was poorer, and so were we. Russ no longer had a government job, but a lower paying, more demanding job as a relief worker.

About Street Kids

We were now living in Nairobi, the capital city of Kenya, with a population in excess of one million. Russ was Somalia Country Director for an international relief agency. Our apartment was in a compound with Asian Indian families. Two guards kept watch over our gate. Russ' office was down the street. He would take periodic flights to Somalia to oversee the project.

This time the street children were unavoidable. They spilled onto the streets of Nairobi, like water flowing over rocks. Some were as young as four years old. They would say, "I am hungry.", or "Will you pay my school fees?"

They all had the standard "uniform": torn, brown, dirty rags that had once been white t-shirts, brown shorts and no shoes. Another part of their uniform, which some hid and some were openly brazen about, was the small plastic containers of "glue". They would put it up to their noses, take a sniff and put it away. Sometimes they held it with their teeth, like a baby bottle. Passers-by would shout at them, "You should stop that glue!" Or, "Why don't you go to school?" and then walk on. The public was smart enough not to try to take it away from them, or a serious fight would have ensued, with much crying and screaming from the younger ones. The glue gave them a "high" to take away the hunger, cold and pain they felt every day. They could pay for this instant gratification for about five cents from the shoe repairmen.

"Why would anyone want to work with street kids? They are so filthy and dirty. I couldn't work with them." This was the sentiment mostly heard about street kids. Expatriates liked to mention their run-ins with the street kids. There were many stories passed around about attempted robberies by street boys. Another story was of a street boy throwing excrement. A local newspaper reported a man being injected by a needle full of AIDS blood by a street urchin. Most people drove with their cars locked and windows rolled up, even in hot weather, to avoid the outstretched palm of a dirty street kid.

The street kids were different in different parts of the city. Downtown Nairobi had the tougher, older ones and the very young ones. Up the hill were the kids who were most high on glue, oblivious of the traffic as they fought with one another on the street. In the suburb of Westlands, where we lived, they seemed more manageable, cleaner and cuter.

Estimates given of these "Children in Difficult Circumstances" ranged from 5,000 to 10,000, and that was just in Nairobi. Wherever there were garbage dumpsters, the street kids would congregate.

Action

When I heard these stories, I wondered what kind of desperation led these children to do such acts. I wondered if they were really hungry, so I observed them. When someone gave them bread, they would snatch it quickly and devour it like animals. They were indeed hungry. One time I tried giving six packs of milk and six loaves of bread to a boy, and told him to share it with the others. He ran away with it all. I tried taking them to a restaurant so they could get a decent meal, but they would just eat "chips" (French fries) and soda pop. The customers would give us snickering looks and sometimes the manager would come out and suggest we take it "to go". I thought I could pass out some milk or bread whenever I went into a store, but I knew this was only a fleeting, temporary solution. I wanted to wait until after Christmas to do something; what, I didn't know.

The time of decision came when I was accosted by street boy high on glue. I was sitting in the car at a stoplight in downtown Nairobi with my arm out the window. The boy first asked for money, and suddenly pulled at my wristwatch. Fortunately, he didn't get my watch, but the pain of his fingernails digging into my wrist lingered for three days. And for three days I thought about the street kids. Russ was out of town, and I decided to act now, rather than wait until after Christmas.

I went to all the different bakeries in Westlands, asking if they would donate some bread; it was very difficult. Finally, one said he would give the throwaways or leftover bread. I had better luck at the westernized Westlands mall, the "Sarit Centre". The butcher, Gilani, offered ten pounds of bones! The grocer in the same mall offered his leftover vegetables, so together it would be a healthy, robust stew.

Our maid, Pamela, used to empathize with me about the street kids when we would pass them in the car. I asked her if she would be willing to cook a hot meal for them. I needed pots and pans that would serve a large number, and went to one of the big downtown stores and talked to one of the managers. He gave me a discount and some items for free. What I had learned in P.N.G. was being used here in East Africa.

Pamela cooked up a stew, along with the traditional "ugali" (white corn meal cooked with water until thickened), a staple in Kenyan diets. The Kenyans said if they hadn't eaten ugali today, then they hadn't eaten. Whatever was not donated, I gladly paid out of my pocket. All of a sudden, I got cold feet. I didn't want to do this. But the cupboards were overflowing with food and everything would spoil if we didn't go ahead.

I asked our compound's tough, scrappy gardener, Francis, if he would be willing to come with us during his lunch hour to help. I knew that two women couldn't do this alone with the wild street boys. Lunch time was 1:00 pm. Pamela carefully put the stew that was still hot into the pots and pans and we carried them into the trunk of the car. I used a bilum (a large bag made of cloth or plastic that can hold food or babies) that was a gift from a Papua New Guinean to throw all the plates in. I said a little prayer in the car.

We picked out a street corner in Westlands, one behind a petrol station that had some trees and a little grassy area. There was a barbed wire fence surrounding it, which we had to cross over. Soon a crowd formed to see what we were doing.

Francis rounded up ten street boys in the area, and the excitement was rising. Pamela and I took out the food and got it ready on the grass. At first it was chaotic and I was so glad Francis was there to enforce some discipline. I explained to the boys that we were bringing food for them, and would do so regularly. I wanted to sing a song and asked one of the boys to sing. He did and the others joined in. This first time I forgot to pray and when we started to pass out the food it was utter mayhem. Some were grabbing the bread while we were passing out the dishes, some were taking two dishes, and some were grabbing in the pot. Francis got their attention as much as possible, but we were wiped out by the whole ordeal. I thought, "I would never do this again."

However, the next day I realized we needed to have more discipline. Talking with Pamela and Francis, we decided to bring a bucket of water so they could wash their hands first, then they would sit down and we would tell a Bible story. There would be a time of singing and then we would all stand and pray for the food, and then pass out the plates, one by one. I was excited for the next time. It took all morning to cook the food and clean up in the afternoon. I also needed time to get donations. We decided to feed only three times a week-Monday, Wednesday and Friday. We were ready for the next time.

A Plan

Pamela, Francis and I prayed again before we left, which we continued to do throughout. As we came to the same spot as the previous day, we saw no kids. Francis went again to round them up. This time the word was out and there were twenty boys! But now we had a plan. They followed the plan with Francis and Pamela giving instructions. It wasn't smooth, but it was orderly. I told a story and emphasized how much Jesus loved them and cared about them. I told them that most of the food was donated by people who also cared about them. I wanted to feed their spirit as well as their stomachs. After eating, they played with a ball I had bought, and were very happy.

Between the feedings I spent all day going to shops asking for donations of food, clothing, sporting equipment and even a soccer field where the kids could play. Whatever was not donated I was able to pay out of my own pocket. At the time the exchange rate was good and it wasn't too much of a sacrifice. I also walked around the shops asking the fruit and vegetable vendors if they knew of any buildings or lots that might be vacant in order to feed the kids. We had some bites, but the door was slammed shut when they found out it was for street kids.

Volunteers

One day the mother of a friend of Laura's was picking up her daughter at school. I invited her to come visit the street boys. Patti Smithson faithfully came and stayed, as well as brought along milk for the boys whenever she could, which was very welcomed. She eventually sponsored a street boy to go to mechanics school. There were many other things she did that I wasn't even aware of. It was a testament to an Americans' perseverance. She was our first volunteer and she stayed to the end, even after we left Nairobi.

Our neighbors became involved. Our next door neighbor hand made "chapattis" (a fried type of bread) for the boys. Another provided money for medicines the street kids needed. At times the street kids came to our gate, which the neighbors seemed to tolerate pretty well.

Having our program on a street corner meant a lot of "drop-ins". People were interested in what we were doing or wanted to help. Others were looking for a job or wanted help for themselves. People were calling me the "U.N." If they said they wanted to help, I would ask them to bring food. If they came back, I would ask them to tutor the kids before lunch. We had many fine Kenyans who dropped in to help, such as Peter, Moses, Anthony, and Nancy, as well as Asians, German, English, an American priest and a Mennonite couple.

Many people had their own ideas on how to help. Some took a kid straight off the street to a clothing store, and bought him a whole new wardrobe. The next day he was back on the street, in his tattered clothes. When a street boy was given clothes, he would ask a kiosk owner to hold his clothes for when he would make a visit back home, or give it to one of his brothers, or maybe sell the clothes.

One of the absolute delights was when a small British school, Peponi School, had their elementary students' brass band come to the street to play for the street kids. The Peponi school students all had bright white uniforms. They set up their little white chairs for the band members to sit on, got out their instruments, and played a song. The street kids were sitting down in a group, very quiet, looking in awe. The song boomed out on the street and indeed, brass bands should be played outside! After the first song, the students said the name of each of their instruments, which was translated. The street kids asked if they could play another song. Yes, they could. So they played the same song again! The street kids clapped joyfully. That was a day we would all remember!

Some of the other schools offered to help. ISK (International School of Kenya), an American run school, took a group of kids to their campus to learn how to use the computer or play soccer. Other schools also brought their students to spend a day with the street kids.

Karanja

We had many people come and go to see our program. One was a reporter for CNN. Usually people would come and go, so I didn't pay much attention, when one day a tall Kenyan lad with a guitar came up to me with a smile. He asked who we were, and I asked who he was.

"Karanja", he said, "I am a volunteer with "Word of Life", a Christian camp north of Westlands. He had been working with these same street kids. Along with Ndua, a volunteer he had recruited, they had been bringing books and sitting under a tree on one of the major highways (Waiyaki Way), tutoring the kids. They would also play soccer on this same strip of land. So while he was teaching the kids one day, they stopped him and said it was time for lunch. He was surprised and wondered where they were going to get lunch. So the kids brought Karanja to lunch one day! He had a powerful presence among the kids, yet he was only twenty-five years old.

He could organize them in a way I couldn't. He would lead them in singing now, and often had a Christian story or drama to tell the boys. I learned later that he had wanted to take some of the kids to camp, and in order to gain their trust, lived on the streets with them. He ate their food, picked garbage and papers like they did-so they respected him very much. He had been praying for these boys, and then I showed up. So together we worked and I learned everything about street kids from him.

I looked for a proper place for a feeding center, and a fruit vendor told me of an abandoned nursery school close by. It was beautiful and perfect, and I contacted the owner, a woman who had a new nursery school, and said we could use the outside of her property for the feedings, which we did. However, one of the boys from Ngara had stolen a sink from the nursery school. The Westlands boys found out about it, and there was a lot of activity and yelling, until finally Karanja retrieved the sink and spoke to the Ngara boys. They hung their heads. Karanja asked me to speak. I found that expats were often expected to say something. I found a few words to say and Karanja translated. He told me that they wanted me to know they were sorry and would I forgive them. I said of course. The sink was returned. However, the repercussions came the next day, when the owner barred us from coming. We were back on the street corner.

Months later the Reverend of a Catholic church on Waiyaki Way gave permission to use his hall for the feeding center. It was wonderful inside, away from the rain. They could sit at proper tables and eat. We asked for long term permission, and they said they would take it up with the board. The board said no. I asked the church secretary if she knew what happened to our request, and she said a woman nixed the idea. It was the same woman from the nursery school, who also attended that church. This was the first time I felt "knifed in the back".

The first thing I learned was that the boys never used the facilities at the medical clinics in the area, even though they needed medical help for cuts, sprains and diseases. Karanja began taking them himself and waiting with them to see a doctor. Most of the time the clinics were out of drugs, so I tried to find a chemist who could give me a discount. Sometimes I went myself and sat with the boys (at one time there were ten of them) and waited with them, for many hours. I came to realize they there scared to death of shots; yet they put up with so much pain in their everyday lives living on the streets. I learned what "STD" was very quickly, as most of them had it.

Enough

After three months I felt like quitting. The toll was showing on me, Pamela and my family. It was just too much work. I decided I had better add another maid, because it took all day to prepare the food, feed the boys and clean up the kitchen afterwards. Ebby came to work for us. I think she broke at least six irons, the stove periodically, took endless days to iron (which I had to ban her eventually after the seventh iron was broken), and ruined most of our clothes by her hand washing techniques. But Ebby was an encourager. She said I would get everything we needed for the boys. She was our Amelia Badelia wrapped in Christian cloth. The donated food was piling up. We continued and I never missed a Monday, Wednesday or Friday, rain or shine, because the boys were depending on us. Sometimes there were up to 100, right on a street corner of Westlands.

Why are there Street Kids?

In Kenya there were no safety nets like welfare, social security or Medicare. The average monthly wage was $40. With no money, there was no food. Many were lucky to just have one meal a day. Housing in many areas was a one room, tin shack, with no electricity, running water or inside toilets. The whole family slept and ate in that one room. If you were lucky you had a cement floor, and the rain didn't come in through the openings. The cold rain during the rainy season fell in buckets and was chilling to the bone.

Many of the kids' mothers had no legal husband, but many children. To survive, some needed to prostitute themselves for food, rent money or clothing. If there was a man living in the house, he may not care about the other children in the home. He may beat them, send them away or even refuse them food.

School was not possible for many even though legally it was "free. There were fees not only for the school, but for uniforms, books, taking an exam, and whatever whim the teacher or headmaster had imposed. If they did not have any of these, they were often chased away by a teacher or headmaster. One day I saw the assistant headmaster with a 2 by 4, hitting each child waiting in a line. The lessons were in English, so new students had a hard time, if they only knew their tribal language or a little Swahili. Many children missed lunch at school and had no food at home.

Most of the street kids came from single parent homes. Children were often cared for by an older sibling when the mother was away or at work. For example, one family with two kids on the street was being taken care of by the pregnant, teenage sister, in addition to six other siblings in the house. Many mothers said they thought their child was "playing in the field" when, in fact, he was in the streets. Others just threw up their hands. Sometimes their child would be gone for days, and the mother wouldn't know where the child was. Occasionally a mother would come to the street looking for her son, but the boy would refuse to go home. Other times the mother would find out that her child had been picked up by the police when she was ordered to show up in court.

At times a mother encouraged the child to beg on the street. That was her only way of getting food in the house for all the other children. There was one case where the father would drop his two kids off by bus at different locations, then pick them up at night. He then forged his own death certificate so they could go into an orphanage. When the director of the orphanage found out the truth, she sent the kids out, and they landed back on the street, this time to stay. These kids were particularly hardened and showed no emotion.

There was also a pattern of siblings following each other to the street. The mothers on the whole loved their children, but were unable to cope, either because of poverty or their own drug abuse. There was a sense of hopelessness pervading these homes. Some came to the street looking for their kids to see how they were, and brought a change of clothes. Sometimes the kids refused even the clothes and refused the mother's plea to return home. One boy with suspected AIDS refused to go home at all, and he died on the street.

Life on the Street

The boys in Westlands tended to be younger and less hardened than the boys from other parts of town. They were stunted by malnutrition and looked younger than they really were. The ones in Westlands ranged from six years old, to the ones that regularly picked paper, 18-20 years old. The older ones, twelve years and up, would "work". They would take a large flour sack and walk throughout neighborhoods, for paper that later would be weighed and they would receive some shillings. Many boys, once they were no longer "young and cute" couldn't get the desired money or food by begging, would begin this paper route. It took a lot of work during long hours of heavy carrying of the flour sack for these boys working in the rain or searing sun.

The older street boys were usually a negative influence on the younger ones. There was usually one "King", who ruled the roost. Karanja got rid of one "king", who was sexually abusing the boys, but another one sprang up, who was actively selling and encouraging the use of glue. He wouldn't give it up unless we "got him a job".

Even though their life seemed carefree to the public, danger lurked everywhere, in addition to getting hit by passing cars and buses. The main thought for a street kid was food and where to get it. They tended to cluster in the same age group and go around begging. They started early in the morning. They used old tin cans to cook their food and get warm. They huddled together at night to stay warm. Bricks and stones were pillows; blankets were non-existent. Lucky ones had a bit of plastic or cardboard box to cover them if it rained. Dogs, rats, and mosquitoes proliferated in the vacant lots and alleys where they stayed. Trash and paper accumulated as high as termite mounds in their "home". The biggest dangers of all were the older street boys and police raids, which happened especially at night.

Yes, reality was hard for them. They had no shoes; or if they did have shoes, they didn't usually wear them. If someone gave them a new pair, they would usually take it home and leave it there, or leave it with a duka (small store) owner, who oftentimes stole the shoes themselves. Walking all over the streets and in the garbage would bring cuts and open sores. Many times they cut themselves on broken glass or nails. They played soccer without shoes as well.

Street Girls

Another danger to the boys was the street girls. We started getting street girls from town to our feeding program, when it got too dangerous for them to stay downtown. They were being picked up by the police, or being beat up in Ngara, another street kid area. They were very unruly and hard to handle. Karanja said he couldn't take the glue away from them (which was required before they joined our group) because they would scream. We had a pretty well organized group, but the girls were not used to discipline.

The girls would come at night and sleep with the boys for a few shillings, and in return give them STD's or AIDS. Some had never had sex before they hit the streets of Nairobi, while some had never even had their periods. Some were severely gang raped. If they got pregnant, they usually had the baby stay with them on the street. That was one of the more heartbreaking scenes: a street girl giving her toddler glue.

The girls had serious, psychological problems. One girl who showed up was mentally handicapped. She was being picked up by an Asian every night, and then returned to the streets. When we took her home, the place smelled of beer, even before we walked in her home. Her mother made and sold illegal beer. We told her she had just gotten out of jail and had been in town prostituting. Her mom said she had no control over her. I contacted a school for the retarded, but they didn't take kids in to stay overnight. I felt she needed in order to get away from the home situation. The girl was always smiling. Her mother promised to watch her. I asked the mother if she believed in God and she said yes. We prayed in her house and left. Two days later the girl was back on the street. I knew of one reputable shelter for girls, run by a tough German woman, but they were overcrowded. It was difficult to even keep the girls there because they ran away.

We had taken some boys back to Westlands after playing soccer one day when Karanja got out of the car, and walked into "Subima", the place where they slept. After fifteen minutes, he came back with three girls. They had been raped by the boys. We took them to see a doctor who confirmed the rape and prescribed medication. One girl could hardly walk. After getting the prescription, Karanja and I took them to a local restaurant in downtown Nairobi, which caused a stir in itself, but they had a decent meal.

I couldn't figure out how to give them the medicine they needed. I knew if I gave it to the girls, either they wouldn't take it, or they would sell it. Karanja had an idea. He asked the manager of a hotel if he could keep the medicine. The girls could come daily for it. I talked earnestly with the girls about this and said it was an experiment, and if they didn't do this I would never help them or any other street girl again. They did it.

One girl, Elizabeth, hadn't even had her first period. As we were walking to the car, her friend whispered that they didn't have any underwear. I bought them two pairs of underwear and they were so happy. How different we were in the west where we expect to have it all.

I checked on them as much as I could. Pamela and I walked down the alleys in downtown Nairobi and asked the older street boys if they had seen one girl in particular. Two young boys said they would show me. At first we couldn't find Elizabeth. Then I saw her slumped on the sidewalk and not able to move. Her sister was with her, urging her home. We had to carry her by hand to the car and the bus depot. We felt somewhat pleased that we had helped get a street child off the street. Months later I saw her in a photo of actors in a drama by street kid. However later I saw her in court, caught yet again by the police. How long would Elizabeth and girls like her live?

The Boys

I was getting to know the boys and their names: Isaak, Mungai, and Kimani. They all had nicknames for each other. One boy, Muskio, was a favorite of everyone who met him; his name meant "big ears". Sometimes I would only know a boys' nickname, not his real name. The boys were great jokers. One time I had a car full of boys driving through downtown when a matatu (an over packed bus) driver asked me where I was taking the boys. Isaak shouted out in English, "To America"!

There was something different about street boys that made them endearing to me. They were stripped of all pretenses to be civilized yet they showed concern for one another. If a boy was hurt by a bus, passerby, or older street boy, the other boy would rush to my house or to another volunteer to get help. When a boy came back from prison, they would give him some of their food from their plate.

Yet they were great liars too. In Kenya, in order to survive, you have to lie. If you told the truth, you would be beaten, either by your parent, teacher, policeman, or by mob justice. It's a survival technique that is hard for Westerners to accept. So they had many stories, and sometimes they would exaggerate. Sometimes it was hard to believe them, when they did tell the truth. Reality was so hard for them that they would tell the story of a boy being beaten by fifteen policemen and even laughed, or show no emotion at all.

I really enjoyed visiting different parts of town and talking to the street kids. Karanja was always respected, and he would talk and pray with them. They would all get silent and bow their heads, and shake hands profusely as we left. One time Pamela and I bravely went alone to bring food to the street boys in Ngara, because we heard that the police had burned down the plastic sheeting used by the boys for their homes to try and get rid of them. The Ngara boys were tougher and more sophisticated than the "Westies".

Many of the youngest street boys were in the downtown area. One four year old girl held my hand for one block. I never gave them money, but would buy a plate of chips or a loaf of bread. They were dirtier than the Westland boys and very high on drugs. It was even difficult to talk to them as they were so high. It was the most dangerous location to be picked up by police.

Another group was by the Yah Yah Center (a high priced orange mall). Even when Karanja and I brought loaves of bread and milk, there was mayhem. It was a hard bunch to control. I think the extra attention given to the Westland boys by people like Karanja and Ndua helped them, and it showed. The "Westies" were never as tough or as high or stole, like "the townies".

Danger to Street Kids

Pedestrians could be a curse to the boys. I saw a white-haired Brit actually slap a boy across the face. Another time when I was picking up bread at a bakery, the boys came running to me and said this one man was beating up on kids. I followed the man to a fish and chips store, where he was buying lunch. I firmly told him never to beat those kids again. If a thief is caught in downtown Nairobi, "mob justice" may explode and beat the perpetrator to death. I saw instances of the public hitting the boys' head. The public tended to be afraid of street kids, yet often if you just talk to them, you will see a smile spread on their face. Security guards also harassed and threatened the street kids. One boy lost his eye when he was beaten with a club by a security guard. The guard was later "transferred" and not to be found.

Most of the stores in Westlands were run by Asian Indians. They were very good business men, but some had reprehensible attitudes towards the black Africans. There was a crowd forming, so I slowed down to see what was happening. Was it a street kid in trouble? I saw the manager of a shop, slapping the African across his face. I ran up immediately and asked what the problem was. The manager said the African had been cheating him on the milk prices. Apparently when the African delivered the crates of milk, he had been taking one for himself each time. I tried as calmly as I could, to get him to stop hitting and told him I would contact the police if necessary. It was a very tense situation, but I couldn't stand and watch by as an Indian slapped an African.

Somalis in Nairobi

Even working with street kids I came into contact with Somalis. One time a Kenyan street boy needed surgery, and I drove him to a hospital outside of Nairobi. While visiting the boy, he told me about a Somali who couldn't pay his medical expenses. The Italian nuns had ordered him to sleep outside at night without a blanket! I went to see the Somali, and he was in a lot of pain. I spoke to the street boy in English, who translated in Swahili to the Somali, who then spoke Swahili to the street boy, who then translated to me in English! I made it clear that I was not there to help him with his medical fees, but that there was a God who loved him very much. I offered him a Bible in Somali, and he accepted it.

A few days later I went back and talked with him more about the Gospel. He said he enjoyed reading the Bible so much! I went back to Nairobi and went to a nonprofit organization to see if they knew a Somali Christian who could come with me to visit the Somali. I picked up the twenty-something Somali gentleman, who was dressed in a suit and bow tie. We had to stop at the street corner where the street boys were first. This seemed be a bit uncomfortable for the Somali, and then we drove to the hospital. I asked the Somali Christian a few questions to test his sincerity, and he seemed very committed. He talked with the sick Somali at length, then turned to me and said he would like to lead him to Christ. I agreed and thought he was ready too. We did and he accepted Jesus as his Savior. I tried to leave other Bibles with other Somali patients. One elderly gentleman had his hand out, but his son stopped him.

Before I left I talked strongly with the nun who had abused him by making him sleep outside in the cold air without a blanket. She asked me not to return. I did return to check on the Somali, but he had left the hospital.

We seemed to have had a burden and love for the Somali people that I can only explain as the prayers of previous missionaries. Why would Russ have any compunction to go to Somalia in the first place, when his peers and family told him he was crazy? When Russ read a 1984 article by Blaine Harden in "The Washington Post" entitled Perfecting the Mogadishu Saunter, it triggered the switch to Mogadishu, from enticing Cairo, Egypt.

Why was it that we run into Somalis wherever we've gone? Even though there were many Somalis in Nairobi, Kenya I didn't become involved with them, because I was volunteering full time with the street kids. It wasn't until a street boy introduced me to one that I got involved. When we did return to the U.S., we had a surprise waiting for us in Columbus, Ohio.

Meanwhile, there was much more to do with the Westland street kids.

Street boy collecting paper

Feeding street boys

Preparing food for street kids

Happy street boy in new half-way house

Street boys and volunteer

Karanja and Elphas

POLICE IN NAIROBI

Pat

It's better on the streets than at home.
Isaac, a street kid

As in most Third World countries, policemen got very low wages and bribery was a way of life. If you were walking down the street, a policeman could ask you for your papers (passport, driver's license, student I.D., etc.). If you didn't have them, they could demand a "little something", beat you, and/or take you to jail. One could tell how much a policeman succumbed to bribery by his stomach: the bigger the stomach, the more they bribed.

By far the most ruthless, dangerous and damaging threat to the civil rights and well-being of street kids was the police. There were periodic round-ups of street kids by plain-clothes-policemen, usually at night when they were asleep. If there was a big convention, such as The International Monetary Fund coming to town, the police would swoop down and pick up as many as they could. The police would like to get rid of the problem of street children in the city. But the brutality of their methods as well as their judicial system would make even Dickens' novels a piece of cake. The police complained that the street kids harassed the public, interfered with the shopkeepers and were accused of stealing. There was no difference in their minds between a kid and an adult.

My First Encounter with the Police

I had only been working with the street kids for a few months when Karanja told me the police were rounding up the boys. He asked if I could check out Subima, where the Westlands street kids slept at night. Before I went in, I asked a friendly vegetable vendor, Richard, if he would accompany me. He was fairly sympathetic to the street kids, and would occasionally give them produce from his stand.

We crawled under the barbed wire and a fence, and walked into the middle of the plot. It was eerily silent. Usually there were older boys, sitting around talking or smoking, but now there was no one. We called out their names, when suddenly a very short and fat plain clothes policeman came thundering up to me and yelled at me in Swahili.

I replied in English that I was just visiting the boys, but he got hotter under the collar. Richard started talking in Swahili to him, but the cop ignored him, focusing his verbal abuse onto me. Suddenly he shoved me to get me to move, and out of the corner of my eye, I saw some of the street boys sitting down with another policeman. The air was very tense, but I tried to smile at the boys. They looked shocked to see me, but showed no emotion, except in their eyes. The fat one continued to scream and holler at me in Swahili. I told him I didn't understand Swahili. This made him even madder, and he pushed my shoulder a couple of times.

My stomach was in knots, when finally an older policeman came out of the bush. He talked to me in English. He asked me for my ID, which I said was in the car. I always left my drivers license and jewelry locked in the car when I went on the street.

He left and a younger cop started talking to me in English. I explained I was just trying to help the street kids, and he seemed more sympathetic. The fat one had left, and finally, after 15 long minutes, the younger cop said I could go. I asked if the younger street boys and an older, sick boy with AIDS could go with me. He would not release any of the boys and only allowed Richard and me to leave. I looked back longingly at the boys, at each face, trying to remember which ones they were. There was no expression in their eyes now.

Although I was shaking on the inside, I met Karanja again. He asked if we had any old clothes we could give to the remaining boys who had not been caught by the police. He said they would be less likely to be picked up if they dressed better. I rushed home and grabbed some of my kids' clothes. Karanja had been able to keep some of the boys at a church office in the area, and later took them to the Word of Life campground. Russ ran out and bought some T-shirts for the boys as well. We also drove some of the boys to the Word of Life campground. These kids were free, for the time being. Karanja told them to stay out of Westlands for a while, but gradually they all came back. The better clothes would help the boys for a while to not get picked up by the police, but it only took a day or two for the shirts to get dirty, and be a target of the police.

The boys caught in a round-up would normally be charged with vagrancy. One time I went to the Parklands Police Department to try and get one of the boys out of jail. The police chief harangued me for an hour, while the street boy stood still in the room. I nicknamed this cop "Idi Amin" for his size, mouth and ruthlessness. Pounding his fist on the desk, he declared "War on the street kids!", and then harangued for an hour about how I was helping "thieves" get stronger by feeding them. I didn't think he was waiting for a bribe; he was enjoying making the street boy stand for a long time, while yelling at me. I pointed out the sign up behind him. It was John 3:16. He didn't even turn around. I realized this was going nowhere, so I got up to leave. The boy was sent back to jail. Idi Amin told me not to come back. Indeed, eighteen street boys were arrested shortly thereafter.

Another time the police had picked up ten boys. We went back and asked if we could feed the boys lunch. It was probably the only meal they would get while incarcerated.

They were put into a cell with adult criminals. There were no beds, blankets or food. They were lucky if they could get a bar of soap.

The police station was supposed to report to the parents that their child was arrested, but this did not always happen. If the mother found out her child was in the police station (usually through another street child), she may attempt to get her son out. It didn't happen that often, especially if the boy was a repeat offender. Before they were sent to court, they were often beaten.

On certain days, the arrested street kids were driven to court from the police station for sentencing. One time the police called me to come over to the police station, ostensibly to get a kid released. What they really wanted was for me to drive the street kids to court, as they had no vehicle. I complied in order to give the kids some bread and milk. Afterwards, I told the police I would not help them drag kids to court again. They did call again, but I refused. Also, I was never successful in getting any of the street kids released from these police stations.

After being caught, it could take weeks before they were sent downtown to the courthouse. On certain days the street kids were taken from the different police stations to the court house downtown for a hearing. There were literally truck loads of them, with policemen carrying guns, as the children got off the trucks and into their next hell-hole. They were dropped off in an ally behind the courthouse, which was near the Boy Scout office and a local theater group. The neighborhood looked normal; however, it masked the terrible conditions inside the courthouse holding cells.

All the street kids were housed in two or three bare, large rooms, boys and girls together. Many were cold and hungry. The only toilets were outside, and the kids needed permission to use them. They slept on the bare cement floor with no blanket, and had only the clothes on their backs.

When the eighteen were arrested, we brought lunch for them at the courthouse. We were allowed in to feed them, but only our eighteen kids. Three children were there whose mother had tried to kill them. When they asked us for food, we gave it to them. We felt good after we left knowing the boys had some nourishment to help them through their ordeal. However, the boys told us later they were beaten very badly after we left for having been fed and helped by a "mzungu" (white person).

The first time I went to court to see if I could help the boys, Karanja and I talked to the judge beforehand. The judge was a small man. He was handicapped and used steel crutches. I marveled at this man and what he had to go through to get to where he was now, a judge. I thought he must have been very tough to get to the place he was today. He had a small Bible on the table. The street kids laughed when we told him he was a Christian, as they faced a judge harsher than King Herod. He said he would release the boys on the condition they were released to Karanja and me. That meant we were responsible for them if they did go back on the street. We were desperate and said, "Yes." The trouble was, when they did go back on the street, we couldn't ask the judge again to release them.

Before the judge came into the hall, the children were herded in and seated on hard benches, or on the floor. There could be hundreds in one day. Some were as young as three years old, and some as old as sixteen. They huddled together against the cold. The windows were open and a cold draft came through. They had the dirty rags on in which they were arrested. A Masaii boy just had a loin cloth around his body. Some talked quietly among themselves, but most just had a strange stare on their faces. Some of the kids were there just because they were "lost".

Three or four caseworkers sat facing the judge with their backs to the kids. They were well dressed and well spoken. The proceedings were in English. They would give their recommendations to the judge. Sometimes the judge would ask a question of the youth. I was invited to sit behind them one day while waiting for the judge. One of the caseworkers suddenly grabbed a street girl and twisted her ear. When she released the girl, she sat in a corner and quietly cried.

The relatives of the street kids stood in the next room, separated by an open door. There were no places to sit. They had to wait until they heard their child's name. However, from the back of the room, it was impossible to hear the bailiff, and their child could be sentenced, just because the parent was "not there". I finally asked the judge if the parents could come inside the courtroom. He said yes, but only a few came in and stood by the door. This showed that the parents were intimidated by the proceedings.

One of the street children started crying when he saw his grandmother. The judge let him go up to his grandmother and she held him, but his wailing got even louder. The judge finally had an officer pull the boy away. I started crying and couldn't stop. The case worker told me to stop crying. A boy that I knew came up to the judge and the judge said he had run away from the remand home too many times. He had walked sixty miles from Navaisha before getting caught this time. I pleaded with the judge to release him to me. The judge roared, "He is MINE!" He sentenced him again to a distant remand home. As the boy was led out of the courtroom, I whispered, "Try to escape." If they were sentenced to an "Approved School" or a "Remand Home", they were to stay there for years. These were neither schools nor homes. The only way out was to escape.

The usual routine was for the judge to look at the paperwork completed by the caseworker. He then made a determination of what should happen to the child. If a parent was in court, the judge may release the child to them. One time the judge refused to release a boy to his sister. Another time the father came and said he didn't want the son, so the judge sent him back to jail. The "lucky" ones were to be given so many strokes of the whip, which was determined by the judge, and then released. Before they were released, they could be beaten again. One young boy asked me for a penny to avoid being beaten. For a penny, the policeman would pretend to hit him when he was only beating the wall.

After sentencing, the boys were taken out in groups, passing the parents and relatives in the next room. After the court session was over, quite a few parents continued to mill around. They didn't know it was over, or even in some cases, their child was sentenced without them hearing the case. If they may have slipped out for a few minutes and were not in the courtroom, they may have missed the case being called and it was their tough luck.

Karanja and I went to visit some street kids who were assigned to the Approved School about thirty miles from Nairobi. We heard that the boys were very sick. This school was just a bit better than the remand homes. The boys were on the road doing work, wearing bright yellow shirts. These were the only kids that had on clothing different from that from which they had when sent here. Most of the boys had the same rags on that they were wearing when arrested. Some of the kids were working in a small garden, and some were gathering sticks for the cooking pot. They were all thin and looked sickly. The director tried to be helpful and found the boys we were looking for. He said none of the parents ever come to visit the children.

The Home in Hell

Although I had been to court and an approved school, nothing prepared me for visiting a remand home. When the street kids were sentenced to a remand home, they stayed for years. Obviously, it was not a home. Three hundred kids were crowded together in a space designed for eighty. There was no separation between age and sex and the rooms were bare. The staff admitted that there was overcrowding, no blankets, little food and no medicine. The usual conditions of a Third World jail were hard enough for adult criminals, but monstrous for juveniles whose only crime was sleeping on the street. The suffering was real. Those who escaped came back to the streets severely ill with rickets, malnutrition and malaria. They also had wounds from being beaten. The children who escaped go right back on the streets. I asked, "Why don't you go back home?" They have the same answer. "It's better on the streets than at home."

The only bed we saw was in the infirmary. It had no medicine or patients. Kids milled around a common courtyard. When it rained, they would stand around in the holding cells, which was the same place where they slept. Some of the kids slept in the bathrooms. It rained often in Nairobi, and it was a cold rain. Some of the older boys would beat the younger ones. There were no new clothes or even uniforms; they were in the same rags they wore when they were picked up by the police. Those street kids who did work outside the building got brown shorts and a shirt, but soon those were dirty due to lack of washing.

There was absolutely nothing for the kids to do all day. We recognized two boys that we saw in the approved school just a few weeks ago. Now they could hardly walk. One had rickets and both were severely malnourished and had scabies all over their body. We asked if we could come back and bring food and medicine, and the director agreed.

When we returned with food and medicine, we were told to segregate the Westlands group from the others. For some diabolical reason, we had to feed the Westlands boys in the middle of the open courtyard while the others watched. The cold rain drops started falling. The boys lined up to the yells of the school mistress and hardened officers with whips in hand. The staff had one street boy use a stick to beat off the other kids trying to get the food. He would yell and use his stick unmercifully. What happened to his young mind, when he beats these kids who are in the same condition as he? My eyes welled up as I realized how he was being used and abused.

The eyes of these children were dark and passive. They had no hope. Who were their role models? It was raining harder as we passed the food out in the open courtyard. My tears mixed with the rain into their soup, as I handed out the meager bowls. I tried not to show the officials my dismay, as they might not let us come back. We had some leftovers. That way we were able to feed the sickest and the youngest of the others. They were so content with this little bowl of food. Afterwards we formed a group and prayed. We didn't know if the officials would let us back in again.

The local newspapers did a story on the state of the remand homes. After this publicity, their attitude changed. One time we had four cars loaded with food and medicine. This was an effort with other groups. Furthermore, we had an American freelance journalist with us. We were denied entry. As we drove away, I saw the children hopelessly looking at us, as we turned around and left. A few months later, after the publicity had died down, we were able to go back and bring bread to the few who were outside working in the garden.

Adult Prisons

The adult prisons were overcrowded as well but often housed juveniles. New prisoners had to sleep in the room with the toilets. They were often beaten by other prisoners. To visit a prisoner, you had to wait for hours in a line. If you were admitted, you went to a room where the prisoners were on one side and the visitors on the other. The wall came up to your neck, so you could only see their heads and look for the person you came to visit. There were bars above the wall. Then you had to yell over all the other voices.

They usually gave you only five minutes. We tried to bring or buy soap there, otherwise they had none. They all wore white shirts and white shorts. They had no sweaters or shoes to beat the extreme Nairobi cold nights. They were very happy to see us, but I was usually at a loss for words. I was relieved to leave.

What can be done?

Everyone wished the kids off the streets. Yet they always ran away from home. These children had to live like adults, since they had no parenting or nurturing. Their learning processes were terribly stunted. They were so busy surviving that they missed the basic developmental processes and emotional and socialization skills that one normally learned growing up. Psychologists say that children need to feel love, safe and capable. The street boys' method of dealing with problems, whether large or small, was to run away and leave all behind. Their friends were

165

their support and family. Their freedom was the most important factor that motivated them. They only thought of the future in grandiose terms.

What can be done for these children who are living in difficult circumstances? There should be laws protecting their rights, accountability and enforcement of these laws. International pressure should be put on the governments to effect change. There were few if any safety nets like welfare, social security, homes for battered women, or alcohol treatment centers. Children did not have a right to go to school. It was a privilege if you could afford it.

A solution for the street children problem was to help the mother's of street children. If they were given an opportunity to earn a living wage, many of these problems could be solved. New companies are slowly entering into the African market, and this should be encouraged and expanded. Support services for these mothers', like day care and counseling, need to be added as well. A support group for these women would provide friendship, support and encouragement. Being able to provide for their family would raise their self-confidence, provide a safe home environment and sufficient food. Many of the kids come from fatherless home. This is a social and religious issue that should be addressed as well.

When one child suffers, don't we and the nation suffer as well? There is a saying that you can tell the character of a country by how it treats their old people. I think it should be by how it treats their children.

NEW LIFE OFF THE STREETS

Pat

I am so hungry my stomach reached to my back-Isaak

I had just taken Isaak, a thirteen year old street boy, back to the streets after a day at a local swimming pool with the other street kids. This time it was different: it was at night. I parked by Subima, where they slept, and got out of the car. I wanted to hug Isaak and "tuck him in bed", but I just stood there, looked into his deep, brown eyes and said goodbye. That was the point when I wanted to do something more than bring food or clothing, and thought of a group home for some of the boys.

I asked Karanja how much a "room" would cost. He had an aunt who rented rooms out for $6 a month, but with no electricity or running water. We went to see it and there were two rooms attached: one could be their bedroom, and one their schoolroom. His aunt and uncle said it would be ok to rent to former street boys.

Children's Church Ministry

Children's Church was an Anglican denomination in Westlands. It looked like a Swedish House in the mountains. It was made of wood and dark inside. Some of the pews were child-size. At the end of the service, the preacher asked the children what they wanted to pray for. Often they would ask to pray for the poor. They put their words into practice, as church members donated clothes, steel bunk beds, and other items. One private benefactor anonymously donated enough so we could pay for the group home expenses.

One day after the service, a woman with an accent and blonde hair came up to me and said she wanted to volunteer. She was Norwegian, married to a national who was in Parliament. She reminded me of my Australian doctor friend in Papua New Guinea, and I was very happy to meet her.

I wasn't sure how she wanted to volunteer, until she said she was a doctor! She was willing to come onto the street and treat the boys. If the problem was more serious, I could bring the boys (and girls) to her office for treatment, which I did.

I went to Ling for advice and encouragement. She was a very brave lady who had to deal with the government who was in opposition to her husband, including threats to her and her children. Her faith remained steadfast and I feel privileged to have known her. I think some of the best people you can meet are expats. Ling was good to her word.

Ling contacted the Norwegian Ambassador's wife, who sponsored a street boy, Michael, to attend a technical school, contributed funds from their charity event to us, took care of the boys' health needs and donated a sewing machine to the women's group.

Setting up House

We went to many shops in Nairobi, asking for donations. Most of the owners were Asian, and usually they would donate something. We had five boys in mind, initially, and then a boy named George came to my door asking for help. I thought the timing was providential and decided to include him in the group.

On the day they left the streets, Pamela, Ebby and I cleaned the boys up with hot water (their first bath with hot water) at our back porch which was outside. We gave them new clothes to wear. The pick up truck was packed with food, clothing and blankets to take to their new home. When they saw their new home, Macharia and Isaak danced a jig. Even though it was empty with no furniture, they said it would keep the rain off of them. We prayed together in the new home and thanked God for making this possible.

At first I didn't have anyone to stay with them. Karanja's cousin who lived next door would come over and help them cook and tutor them. I knew I had to have an adult stay full time, but who? There was one volunteer, Elphaz, from the Luhya tribe, who came every day to the street feeding. He rarely even asked me for bus fare, and the cousin he stayed with didn't like him working with the street kids. I asked if he would be willing to stay with the boys, and he agreed. For six months Elphaz tutored them in their new home, Uthiru Boys Paradise Centre. Later Alice Akhura came as a cook. However, there were challenges.

Insight into the Characteristics of Street Kids

The hardest thing for a street boy to give was his freedom. That was all they had while living on the street; they may not have had food or warm clothing, but they could come and go as they pleased. The only rules were for survival, which they had been able to do, up to this point. Would they be able to see the long term benefits of staying off the street and living there with rules?

Another characteristic of street children were that they liked instant gratification. If they wanted something, they took it. They would worry about getting more the next day. They also didn't have the concept of working hard, for years if necessary, and having to wait to get what they wanted or needed. Karanja asked them once what they wanted to be. They answered, "A pilot, a doctor, president, etc." His next question was, "How are you going to get it?" Their answers were unrealistic, such as "I just want it.", or "I'll pray for it." They had no conception of what it took to try and succeed and try, try again.

Street kids were very social. Their friends, after glue, were probably the most important thing to them. They were great story tellers and loved to tell stories. They tended to run around with the same age group, and shared the same experiences and troubles. Adults were usually seen as hurting them or telling them what to do. They don't have school or their own families who can help them feel good about themselves. When we took these boys off the street, we took away a lot of their social life, and therefore, what they felt good about themselves. We hoped that what we were offering would take the place of it, because we all have a need to be loved.

Street kids got angry very easily, especially if they did not get what they wanted. Some would pout if they didn't get a donated shirt they wanted, and others would run away. Running away was often used to deal with problems or situations they wouldn't or couldn't deal with. Instead of telling a parent or adult they were having problems, they would keep it to themselves and literally run away, just as they ran away from their families.

The boys had a lot of time on their hands and were meeting some of the other neighbors, who were almost like themselves, but hadn't gone to the streets. The boys would be ridiculed too, for being street kids and called names. Even though the boys had named their home, "Boys Paradise Centre", it was just one level up from Sabima, until, finally, we were asked to leave.

It took two months to find a new place. George and Isaak asked to be circumcised, which is a major ritual in Kenya. We found a clinic nearby and drove the boys home to heal. They were supposed to stay inside and not supposed to see people, especially girls. Isaak healed quickly, but George had problems and took longer. We bought a new "kanga" (a cloth Kenyans wear) for them, and fish, as Isaak had requested, for dinner.

Elphaz and I drove around the outskirts of Nairobi looking for a new home. We stopped by the roadside in Uthiru, fifteen minutes from Nairobi, and Elphaz spotted a real house, with a wood frame and tin roof. There was a living room, two bedrooms and a small room for the kitchen, with a charcoal stove. We talked to the landlord, but did not specify they were street kids. After six months off the street, they looked like regular kids; they had put on weight and wore decent clothes. It cost $20/month, with no running water, electricity or indoor toilet. I offered to pay a deposit, as well as the first month's rent, and we signed the papers. We packed everything in a pick up truck from the old house, and joyfully moved into Uthiru.

Now the boys were ready for school. Elphaz talked to the Headmaster at the public school in Uthiru, and they could go there for 5,000 shillings each. Books, uniform and lunch were extra. We found sponsors for them, but finances were mounting up and up. The boys looked shiny in their new uniforms and seemed very pleased. However, they would be placed in classrooms with kids much younger than they. Charo had been taught by Ndua and Karanja how to read when he was on the street, but he knew little English, and all the classes were taught in English. He towered over the other kids, but made very big attempts. During recess, some of the boys, Isaak, Mungai and Machairia would play with the boys their own age. They didn't want to be known as street kids anymore.

One day George didn't come back from school. Elphaz went looking and looking for him and tried to contact his relatives. The boys prayed for him at the home. Three months later I saw George coming towards me at the street program on Waiyaki Way, dirty, in rags and high. The first thing he did was give me his bottle of glue. I went to my car parked nearby, sat inside and cried. I kept his glue bottle to remember.

Much later I found out he didn't want to go to school. He was the first chosen to go to school because of his good behavior, but I had never asked him if he wanted to go to school. Apparently his father had forced him to go to school. I didn't know. We replaced him later with another boy who was sponsored by an American teacher at the International School of Kenya. But one lost is like one hundred. George was later diagnosed as probably having AIDS, but he refused to go home. As far as I knew, he was still on the street or dead. One day when I was taking Pamela home, her frustrations spilled over too, and she said, "Why waste money on these street kids, why not give money to kids who aren't on the street so they could go to school?!" I was silent. I wondered the same thing too.

I decided that I would not go looking for a boy. If he chose to leave, then that was final. He would never be allowed to come back to live. One day Isaak found an old street friend who had a bike. He was gone for one week. Elphaz found out he had ridden the bike back to his aunt's, a thirty minute car drive away. I told Elphaz to bring him back. Just as he saw him, Isaak said he was coming back. I thought there was more to Isaak because of this incident, but no one could really get close to him.

I forbade corporal punishment on the boys, since they had had so much of it either at home, on the streets, in police station and/or the remand home. We instituted rules and punishments, such as digging up weeds. Macharia was very good at this, taking his punishment. But he began spending time with other boys know to have drugs and meeting girls by the outdoor water faucet. Some of the mothers complained to Elphaz that they were afraid for their daughters. Macharia was caught one day with drugs, and I kicked him out for a week. When he came back, he was broken, and we almost lost him. It was a very hard punishment for him, and he missed school that week as well. He did complete two school years and then had to leave the home because of his age.

Holidays were an especially difficult time for Elphaz and the boys. They would get very bored. Word of Life Institute held camps during the holidays and the boys could go there during their breaks. They also had a membership to the YMCA and swam in the pool, thanks to Beth, a great American volunteer.

During the trial for a police reservist who had killed Simon, a street boy, I had two eyewitnesses, Kimani and Minor stay at the home in Uthiru. After the trial, I rented two more rooms near Uthiru for them, as a safe house. Another boy, Shorty, also stayed in the safe house. He spoke English very well, and a neighbor offered to tutor the boys. One problem was that these guys were in their twenties and difficult to handle. The day I was supposed to bring all the boys to introduce them to Children's Church, one had thrown boiling water over another guy. I told them to get dressed and that we were going to Children's Church. They complied and I talked to them later and they seemed sorry.

Now there were two homes, school expenses, supplies, food, clothing, medical care, and bus fare, in addition to the cooking and feeding on the street. Children's Church had continued to support this ministry monthly and an anonymous donor gave $1,000 periodically. We also received some donations from churches in the U.S., but it still didn't cover all the costs of the homes.

A Stranger comes to visit

One day an unknown woman came to the feeding on the street. She would lead the singing, and had a strong personality. Although I could offer her no job, she came quite a few times. One day she handed me a piece of paper and said they could help me. I looked at the paper and it was Terre-des-Hommes, a Dutch assistance group. Elphaz and I wrote the proposal and met with the Director. He said the budget was too large, so we downsized it. It was to include the two group homes, the formation of a new one, and sponsorship for twenty kids for school for those kids living at the home, as well as a self-help group. The proposal was approved, but they wanted it to be registered.

Meeting the Mothers of Street Children

I had wanted to do something for the mothers of street children. I knew that this would be the source of the problem and the source for a solution. I had visited in their homes and seen how desperately they lived. I wanted to give them some hope and encouragement.

Kangemi was the slum where many of the kids came from. We met with a man who worked with a church there. He was willing to contact the mothers of the street kids, and planned a meeting in the local school. Many women came, some from far away and others whose kids were not street kids. We had to limit it to those who already had kids on the street, abut this was easier said than done. I wasn't sure what to do with the group once it was formed, and I knew Beth would have some great ideas.

Beth

I met Beth when the guard of our compound told me there was an American lady who lived three houses down and who wanted to help the street kids. Dr. Beth Swadener, with red hair, purple dresses and shoes, and a twinkle in her eye, had arrived to do a project on child development with her colleagues. She had a PhD in Education, and was a professor at Kent State, but to our son Ryan, she was "The chocolate-chip lady", because she often brought homemade chocolate chip cookies over to us. To the street kids, she was called "Mama Harakisha", which means "in a hurry, or very busy". Her laughing and smiling face always cheered up the boys.

Beth brought energy, laughter, love, and volunteers to the street. She provided games and books, as well as school and art supplies. She encouraged the boys in art, and scouted for old cardboard boxes which she cut up as "desks".

For the first time we could see kids who had some talent in art. At first they drew matatus (Nairobi buses) and cars. Then they were encouraged to try other subjects, and drew traditional homes, churches, pigs and even a policeman shooting street boys. Beth organized art exhibits at a local tourist shop and at the Sarit Centre mall. She found a place where their work could be exhibited. To prepare for the exhibit, Beth took pictures of the kids, and had them matted on bright colored paper. At one point we decided they needed a cleaner environment in which to do art work, so they came in groups to our home. They even tried to replicate the art I had hanging up in the house.

Beth was a shot in the arm for the ministry and was my right hand. She helped carry the burdens, but always with a smile. Plus, I wasn't alone any more. Beth had lots of ideas.

Beth was the most positive person I knew. Nothing could get her down, for long. She organized art exhibits at a local tourist shop.

The local mall, Sarit Centre, was going to have booths of different street children organizations, and Beth organized it all. I secretly wondered how long this volunteer would last, and there came a test. While at the Sarit Centre, someone stole her wallet. I thought that was the end; she would never be back. But that night we went to visit some of the mothers of street children in their homes. She came back.

Beth and the Mama's

Beth was instrumental in starting the women's group. She was a natural with the mothers of street kids. She brought her university friends to meetings to talk and counsel the women. During the first meeting, the women stood up, one by one, saying what they needed. We explained that the purpose of the group was to help themselves, with assistance from volunteers for needed supplies and materials.

The second meeting they looked very different: the mamas were spruced up and held their heads up higher. My friend, the Norwegian doctor, came and talked about reproduction and family planning. We received a donation of a sewing machine from a woman who had sponsored one of the boys from the group home; it was her birthday money and she wanted it to go to the ladies. Many friends of Beth brought donations of clothing and sewing materials to give to the group.

We saw the need of the women to empower themselves so they could provide for their families. They needed to do something to make an income in order to avoid brothers and sisters of street children joining them on the streets. We wanted to give them the dignity of a productive job and income to develop their self-respect.

Beth Starts a New Home

Beth introduced Thai-dye to the boys in the group home, as well as paid their membership to the local Y and swimming pool. She found sponsors for the school fees for the boys in the home. She bought chickens for them to start a small business. The chickens slowly disappeared, either being stolen or eaten. To Beth, disappointments were not in people but in actions.

One of the last gifts she gave before her year was up in Nairobi was to pay for the starting of a third group home. This would be for older boys who showed talent in art. They were to stay at the Vavuum Art Center in Kiambu. They were trained in sculpture, woodcarving, and arts and crafts by a Kenyan artist, Morris Foit. The boys did their own cooking and washing. To this day, Beth helps current Kenyans and expatriates who are working with street kids. Other donors to the group homes included Children's Church, local banks, hotel industries, supermarkets, butcheries and individuals.

Simon

Pat

Ever since an IMF (International Monetary Fund) meeting was held in Nairobi in the summer of 1994, there seemed to be more pressure to get the kids off the street. The only way the government knew how was to arrest them. The kids were agitated when I arrived at the feeding center; they said a street boy had been shot. I assumed he had been taken to the hospital, which is what usually happened. After we put the pots and pans in the car, Pamela told me he had died! I asked which boy he was. His name was Simon.

The headlines in the newspaper said, "Street Boy Shot". I didn't want him to be a nameless, faceless street boy. I called the local newspaper and told them I knew his name and even had a photograph of him eating at our "center". The media picked up the story and publicized it even more. He was no longer a nameless, faceless street boy.

I met Simon's parents in the newsroom of a local paper, The Nation, along with a politician who was outraged by the case. The boy was shot five times by an Indian police reservist (a part-time citizen who can carry a gun) for allegedly stealing a rear-end light from a car. The reservist chased the boy, shot him, and kicked him in the stomach while he lay on the ground. He then spit on him and called him a "stupid African". There were many witnesses, and public outrage.

I found out from the street boys that two of our regulars had been with Simon at the time of the shooting. I found them in Ngara, and asked if they were willing to testify in court to what they saw. They agreed, but first we went to the newspaper to give their report. I then took them to a lawyer who took down these eyewitness statements. However, the politician was not pleased with this lawyer, who was Indian (and who was very well known and respected) and doing this for free, and at a risk to his own safety.

The politician chose another lawyer. I told him I had no money to pay a lawyer and that we already had an excellent lawyer with a good reputation who was working for free. I tried to convince Simon's parents that they could choose the lawyer, but they were overwhelmed by the politician and chose his lawyer.

In the newspaper the next day, the lawyer chosen by the politician was named as the lawyer who was taking the case. I wasn't sure how to proceed, now that the lawyer I had contacted was out of the picture.

Right before the trial was to start, I decided I had to bring the eyewitnesses forward. I found one of the original witnesses, plus two others who were willing to go to the Kasarani police station to give a statement. At first, the officer in charge said the government had enough evidence for their case, and wouldn't need their statements. I told them that once they heard their testimony, they would be convinced they were excellent witnesses. I think he was nervous about them being street boys. Then he said it was too late to take new evidence; I cited the O.J. trial and how new witnesses were called all the time. He finally agreed. After taking the statements, the police said they would expedite the process and sent the statement to the attorney general's office. The attorney general had the authority to determine whom to call as witnesses.

I then visited the lawyer for the government who was prosecuting the case. He was very wishy washy about these boys testifying, so I tried to convince him. He said he could not make the decision, but sent it up to the Assistant Attorney General. We were able to get in to see him. He was sitting at his desk with piles of legal briefs, almost higher than he was. I quickly explained who I was and what I had come for. He had not read the statements, but said he would. I left not knowing for sure if he would use these boys to testify.

Trouble in Westlands

Soon after Simon's photo had been in the paper, a policeman came to Russ' office and said, "Are you Pat Wolford's husband? Can you show us where she is at the traffic circle?" Russ got in the car with the policeman and an Indian to lead them to the feeding location at the traffic circle. Russ, of course, knew what had been happening. He complied with their request, but he didn't talk nicely to them. He must have scared off the Indian, because he got out of the car before they reached the traffic circle. Russ always wondered if this Indian was the murderer. The policeman wanted to take me to a police station and take my statement. I refused and suggested we sit in my car which was my "office". I knew very little, except that Simon came to our feeding occasionally. Right before the trial, I got a notice to appear in court as a witness for the prosecution!

This was a time when the police were doing extra pick-ups of the street kids, and we moved our feeding centre to avoid them. One day I was riding in a Rosslyn Academy school van with some other moms. I didn't know them, so I introduced myself. One of the women spoke up and said, "Pat Wolford? You are Pat Wolford?!" Apparently her church was praying for me and had my name written on their blackboard, Pray for Pat Wolford. They had a break-in at their church office and the police came to make a report. One of the policemen saw my name on the board and blew up, "What are you doing with that woman? Why are you working with her?" These were policeman from a police station I had never been to and did not know any of them. She said she would pray for me; I needed it.

The police reservist had three, expensive lawyers working for him: one Indian, one black African and an old Greek lawyer who came out of retirement to take the case. The Greek lawyer, by the way, had never lost a case. He was known for his courtroom antics and did his best to get his client off. I had heard that the defense was going to say that Simon had a knife, and that Simon was not sixteen years old as his father alleged, but over eighteen years old. This last part bothered me, because there were rumors that he was indeed not sixteen. Some of his "age mates" (boys who were circumcised the same time he was) were over eighteen.

Simon's Funeral

On the day of the funeral police were rounding up kids, especially downtown. There wouldn't be a riot. There were only a few of us that arrived at the mortuary downtown. At first they wouldn't let us in, but then the politician arrived and waved me in. Some of the boys had been in to dress Simon for the open casket. Someone asked if we should have a short prayer. I replied, "No, he lived outside and we'll pray for him outside."

They brought the casket out and put it in the back of a beat up truck, which was going to take it to the place of burial in Thika. The local Westlands vendors had donated flowers. Only half of his body was covered and we could see his face. Someone pushed me forward to look at him. I gasped, "Simon, Simon". Then his parents came forward and his mother was crying. Suddenly they closed the casket, and the politician asked me to pray, along with the others. My throat was closed up, but I found some words to say, in English.

The family went with the politician in his car, and I left with some street boys and Elphas. Another woman who, according to the papers, was a "friend of street kids" was in another car. That was it as we drove through the city streets.

Once out of Nairobi, we met up with a few more cars, mostly journalists. The road was lined on both sides with policemen for our meager procession. Halfway there, the truck carrying the casket broke down. The politician went to Thika, his hometown, to find another one. I brought out some bread and passed it among the street kids and family members. Finally the politician appeared with another truck.

I smelled other trouble. Along the way there seemed to be more policemen and checkpoints than normal. As we turned to go into Thika, the number of police dramatically increased until we came to a road block of police in riot gear. We were following the politician, and he was yelling and screaming at the police. Someone came back to my car and told me to follow him. Suddenly the politician's car swerved and went around the policemen. Apparently he was going to go the back way to where the rest of the funeral procession was to meet in the town of Thika. I screeched ahead and tried to follow him, but he was going too fast. Along the way I could see men trying to get a lift, but they had billy clubs and I figured they were trouble. As we slowly approached the town, there was a mob surrounding the one restaurant where we were to meet.

I parked a distance from the mob scene, and suddenly tear gas went off. I quickly turned the car around to go the other way. I was shaking with fear, but didn't want to show the street boys, so I tried to make a joke out of it. I didn't even know where to go, but then found the lady who was the "friend of street kids" car, and regrouped at a gas station.

The politician was there, the lady and a few others. I asked if we could go to the burial site, but they said to wait. I was concerned about the safety of the street kids in my car. Finally we began to move and drove out of Thika. We passed a very bumpy road next to a Dole pineapple farm, and drove for another hour. I was glad we had the bread earlier.

Simon's parents' house was a sturdy, block building. It was set out in the country with mountains in the background. There was a tent and some chairs for us to sit on, and we waited. More and more people came, walking long distances. Then the other politicians came. Suddenly I noticed Simon's parents weren't there. I mentioned this to the politician, and he seemed surprised. Later I learned he had sent his car back to Thika to try and find them. They finally arrived.

The ceremony began; yet, it was more like a politician's rally than a funeral. One by one the politicians stood up and harangued against this injustice by an Indian. Then it was my turn to speak. I said I knew Simon to be quiet, but he would always help without being asked. Then I said the reservist needed to pay for the consequences. Then I asked, "Can we forgive him?" There was a resounding "NO!" I was taken aback for a minute, so I said, "That's right. We can't, but we have to let the God that is within us help us to eventually forgive; otherwise the bitterness will just grow." I didn't know how this was received, especially by the family, but I thought that's what I wanted to get across.

There were more political speeches and then it was starting to get dark. I was ready to go back home, but one of the volunteers with me urged me to go to the burial site. It was in the plot right next to the house. Someone gave me a shovel; I wasn't sure what to do with it, so I gave it to the volunteer, and she shoveled dirt into the hole. I then retrieved the shovel and shoveled dirt in. The air was covered with sand and dirt. I took the donated flowers and passed them out among the street boys who had carried the casket. They then threw the flowers on the casket. The funeral was over, but in the back of my mind I still wondered why Simon left this place, a beautiful shamba in Thika.

I did go back to visit his parents once. They told me that after the funeral, no one came. In fact, they didn't even know when the trial was set, so we informed them of the details. The next day a policeman came and also gave them the details.

Getting Ready for the Trial

Two of the witnesses I had brought were going to testify, but I didn't know which day. So each day I would find them on the street, hoping they weren't high on glue. I finally had them stay in a "safe house", and brought them to court to wait for them to be called. Finally on the third day they were called.

The prosecution was having problems. Their witnesses were messing up. The first one even pointed to the wrong man when asked who the reservist was. I also noticed that the Greek lawyer, Georgiadis, made the witnesses nervous. Frankly, he made me nervous. I told the street boys to tell the truth and speak in their mother tongue (Kikuyu), rather than try English or Swahili.

The court room was packed everyday. I sat facing the witness stand so I could smile and show signs of encouragement to my two witnesses. Kimani was the first witness. He was a very different kind of guy and had a bit of a high-nasally voice. Georgiadis was taken aback by him and even asked him if he was always like that. Kimani didn't know what he was getting at. But then Kimani started telling the judge exactly what he saw, and there was total silence in the courtroom. You knew he was telling the truth and had been there. The next witness wasn't as strong, but I thought he could hold up. In his own quiet way he told what he saw. I thought they performed very well, and held up to Georgiadis' antics.

The next day the prosecutor told me Georgadis had complained that I was coaching the witnesses and to sit somewhere else! I didn't want to give him any excuses, so I sat on the other side, and gave him a dirty look. The second witness was different from the one I had originally taken to the first lawyer. So when Georgadis asked this witness if he had talked to the first lawyer, he said no, and Georgadis was taken aback. Where had Georgadis gotten that information? The trial lasted two weeks, and I was on the stand briefly. I only had the opportunity to state how I knew Simon.

There were three "Assessors", which were like a jury. They sat through the trial and gave their verdict at the end. They may or may not influence the judge with their decision. One time outside the court I went up to an Assessor and asked what an Assessor was, since it was unfamiliar to me. We started talking, until Georgadis came up to my face and said, "You are NOT to talk to the Assessor while the trial was going on!"

The day for the verdict came. We looked for street kids to take, but only found a few. The judge was explaining his reasoning of his verdict before stating it, so Karanja and I slipped out to bring some more boys. We found them, but it was so crowded I couldn't get back in the courtroom. I was standing on my toes trying to see and hear. I had a camera in my pocket. An African standing next to me was saying, "Yes!" in a loud voice to everything the judge was saying. At first I stared and then I started talking back to him. People were shushing me and we were getting louder and louder. Finally the judge gave his verdict: "Not guilty." I expected mayhem. It was quiet in the courtroom.

I left stunned. Some of the street boys came out with me and Karanja found the others. TV and newspaper people were asking others for a statement. I said, "It was a sad day for street kids." Then I remembered Psalm 26:10, which I had read that morning: "in whose hands are wicked schemes, whose right hands are full of bribes".

I walked to the truck I used to carry the street boys, with Russ' work emblem on the side, and noticed the TV crews following us. Suddenly I told the boys to get some of the flowers close by, the beautiful bougainvilleas, and put it all over the car. To me, it was like a funeral. Suddenly Kimani started singing a Kikuyu lament; was it a funeral dirge?

We slowly drove down Waiyaki Way. I didn't know where to go; some of the boys were from Ngara. But I drove to Westlands, by the tree where we always sat. I wanted to be together with them.

Later, Karanja told me the boys wanted to get revenge, but Kimani and Karanja said no, and it worked. There was no action taken by the street kids in response to this verdict. Later we heard rumors that the judge allegedly took $US 20,000.

I immediately put the two witnesses in the safe house and kept them there for a while. They were brave and courageous. Ndua had counseled them also not to run if the police yelled, "Stop!"

After the Trial

This same reservist who got off was a prime suspect in the murders of five other street boys in Ngara. (The Daily Nation, 12/6/95) Guess who his lawyer was: Mr. Georgiadis.

Street kids were and continue to be, even more in danger. * One boy in Ngara was hit by a matatu and died. The mob took over and burnt the matatu. The next day the police rounded up all the street kids in Ngara and arrested them. A boy named Chege was beaten to death while in police custody. Again we had two eyewitnesses who were willing to testify. The day after I brought them to talk to the lawyer, who was going to take the case for us for free, one was beaten by fifteen policemen on the street. He was beaten so badly he could not walk. We were able to find a pathologist who agreed to be present at the autopsy, in order to give them a legal standing. It was still to come up for trial. Then another street boy in town was beaten up and killed by mob justice in 1994.

Meanwhile, my application for registration for Westlands Children's Ministries was still being held up. After this trial it was denied because it would hurt the "peace and order" in Kenya. According to the Attorney General, Amos Wako, in The Nation, they refused to register it for "security reasons: in the interests of peace, welfare and good order." I immediately filed a formal appeal, to no avail.

Conclusion

Life was hard in Africa. Many struggled every day, just to get food in the average home. It was doubly hard for street children. Their plight was grim. There were efforts by some to help them. I had seen smiles on the faces of these children as they were given hot, nutritious food and medicine they needed. After they ate, they played, like children.

I had seen how street boys had been given hope and confidence as they were given schooling and training. One boy said, "I am so hungry my stomach reached to my back." His friends laughed because they knew what he was talking about. I saw a few examples of how the establishment could be influenced to show more tolerance and support for the street kids. I also saw mothers of street children and how they had their view of life changed by giving them self-respect through training and support. We can make a difference in someone's life. Otherwise, it is a death warrant for many street kids.

www.kidstokidskenya.org.-see how Children's Church is continuing to serve.

Simon's Burial

VERANDA OF THE NORFOLK

Russ

Hemingway slept here. Robert Ruark wrote about it, and Teddy Roosevelt launched his famous safari from the front door. Lions could be heard at night in the papyrus swamp across the road, in the location now occupied by the Nairobi University. The Norfolk Hotel, founded in 1904, is the oldest hotel in Nairobi.

The first place we headed after our first Sunday church service in Nairobi was the Norfolk. The kids enjoyed the food from the children's menu. One of the items was called "Millie, Molly, and Mandy". Pat and I enjoyed steak and kidney pie and the ambiance. Some of the patrons were obviously tourists in crisp, new khakis. Some were undoubtedly seasoned expatriates, and it was fun to guess the origin of the crowd in between. Some may have been the sons of the old, white settlers; but I've been told that they go where the beer was cheaper.

You never know whom you may see at the Norfolk. One night Pat and I put the kids to bed and slipped out for dessert and coffee on the veranda of the Norfolk. We noticed a large number of people in formal dress coming and going from the lobby. There was also an uncommon number of white Range Rovers pulling up at the front door. Pat recognized one of the men getting into a Range Rover as the British High Commissioner, and she said, "Fergie's in town." Soon we recognized the Duchess of York making her way through a crowd of well-wishers at the entrance. I didn't know whether to ask for her autograph, and Pat said to be cool and not act like a slobbering American. No one else was asking for her autograph. The duchess gracefully entered the waiting, white Range Rover. Her red hair was almost auburn in the Nairobi moonlight, and her lovely figure was outlined by the candlelight from the veranda of the Norfolk Hotel.

When making an engagement for lunch or dinner, the most expedient venue was the veranda of the Norfolk. You could always get a seat in a good setting. The veranda was known as the office for people who had no office. Whenever the Somalia team leader came to Nairobi, and we wanted to have a serious talk, we went to the Norfolk. When the Somalis came to town, the Norfolk was a mandatory stop. I wanted to show them where Karen Blixen and Farah Aden met, but they didn't know who those people were. This didn't surprise me too much. What did surprise me was that all of the Somalis ordered fish. In fact there is a Somali saying about a person who doesn't tell the truth, that he talks like a person who eats fish. The Somalis from the Juba River Valley ate fish. I even knew some Isaaqs and Dulbahantes in Mogadishu who were in the fish business. Again, Somalia was full of contradictions, but I later learned that Somalis eat fish if they are in a place where the meat would not be halal (butchered and prepared in the Muslim way).

I was sitting on the veranda of the Norfolk one night. A white Range Rover pulled up, but Fergie didn't get out. The evening crowd of diners had left. It was the rainy season, and the breeze was damp and chilled. I pulled the collar up on my jacket and walked to the truck. Simba wasn't lurking on the sidewalks of Nairobi University, but I felt the bite of the night air as I fumbled for the key to the ignition. Another night was passing by. It was closing time on the veranda of the Norfolk.

It was also the close of another era of our lives. We felt a sense of accomplishment in working on issues that were bigger than we and in having a part in affecting events and communities in a good way. The things we did in the middle of turmoil in East Africa affected our lives, and we remained connected with those people and places. We were sentimental about the successes and failures in Mogadishu and the joy of building houses in Port Moresby. We remained committed to helping refugees and being advocates for the underdog.

The family at Nairobi Game Park Ryan, Laura, Pat, Katie, Russ

Buffalo and Egret Nairobi Game Park

Zebra at Nairobi Game Park

APPENDIX

Somali Clans
Perfecting the Mogadishu Saunter,
by Blaine Harden, Washington Post, 1984
Summary of Somali History
Political Map of Somalia
Clan Map of the ethnic groups of Somalia
Street Map of Mogadishu with U.S. Embassy buildings
Map of Papua New Guinea
About the Authors

SOMALI CLANS

The patriarchs of the Somali clan system are the Darod, Hawiye and Dir. They arrived on the Horn of Africa around 1200 AD. They were Arabs and brought Islam with them, but they didn't replace the Somali language with Arabic. Clan lineage is a complicated matter. Dir arrived on the Horn of Africa first, followed shortly by Darod and Hawiye. These were the patriarchs of the nomadic clans, known as Samaale.

The agricultural clans of the south are known as Sab. The group that makes up the agricultural clans includes Rahanweyn, Digil and Mirifle. These clans are likely a joining or mixing of the various other Somali clans with coastal people of various origins. In fact, Rahanweyn in one dialect means "people who come together". A detailed illustration of the clan families is included in the Appendix.

The nomadic Samaale clans have 4 major nomadic groups:
1. Hawiye
2. Darod
3. Dir
4. Isaaq

SAMAALE-Nomadic Clans

1. Hawiye
   1. ABGAL-Mogadishu area
   2. HABAR GIDIR-Central Somalia, controlled Southern Mogadishu
   3. MURUSADE-Northern Mogadishu
   4. DAGODI-Ethiopia, Northern Kenya
   5. HAWADLE-Belat Wein
   6. GARREH-Northern Kenya

The greatest concentration of this clan family is found in the central regions of Somalia.

2. Darod
   1. MAREHAN-President Siad Barre, Central Somalia and Bardhera
   2. MAJERTEEN-North east Somalia
   3. OGADEN-Ethiopia, Western Somalia
   4. DULBAHANTE-North, between Isaaq and Majerteen
   5. WARSENGELI-Northwest

Darod arrived on the shores of Somalia after Dir and Hawiye, but his clan has been prolific.

3. Dir
  1. AFAR-Northwest
  2. AJURAN
  3. GADABURSI
  4. SHEEQAAL
  5. GAALJEEL

Various ethnographers and Somalis say that the nomadic tribes of northern Kenya and the Tutsis of Central Africa are from Dir's lineage.

4. Isaaq
  1. HABAR JELO
  2. HABRAWAL
  3. HABAR YONIS

A major clan of the Northwest - Isaaq are Dir, but they are big enough and significant enough to be considered a fourth major clan.

SAB Clans-The Farmers and Agriculturalists

The sedentary clans of the Southern riverine regions are known as the Sab. The primary clan group is the Rahanweyn. Rahanweyn means "people who come together", and they are an amalgamation of all the Samaale clans, as well as Bantu and coastal people. These are the non-nomadic people who mix livestock herding with farming.

SAB-Farmer and Agriculturalist Clans

1. Rahanweyn-Farmers in Saakow, between the two rivers
  1. GELEDLE
  2. LAYSAN
  3. MALIMWEYN

2. Digil and Mirifle-In Afgoye, took part in stick fights

OTHER Clans

1. Midgan-Considered outcast due to a legend about eating pork
2. Bantu-formerly slaves, agricultural workers and from other parts of Africa
3. Coastal-Mix of Arabs, Persian traders and Somali
  1. BENADIRI
  2. REER BARAWE
  3. MARKA

PERFECTING THE MOGADISHU SAUNTER

was piqued by this article.

Perfecting the Mogadishu Saunter

MOGADISHU, Somalia — Sharks prowl the surf that breaks gently beside this desert city. They were lured to Mogadishu's beach about six years ago when the Russians, then patrons of Somalia, built a seaside slaughterhouse just north of town. Several times a year these sharks, excited by the blood and offal that slithers down the beach and into the sea, eat citizens of Somalia.

At the Anglo-American Beach Club, a seedy, hospitable establishment on the beach, expatriates spend their afternoons drinking Danish beer, sunbathing, snoozing, not swimming and reminiscing about shark attacks.

"With my own eyes," testified a British geologist who works for the United Nations in Somalia, "I've seen three people killed. One had his leg bitten off, another both legs and three months ago I saw one young man reach for a football that had been kicked into the surf. He lost both arms up to the elbows."

An American diplomat confirms the report of the youth who lost his arms (and later died) fetching a soccer ball. The Somali ministry of health says there have been two fatal shark attacks on the Mogadishu beach in the past seven months.

"You can always tell when there's been an attack," said the geologist, who did not want to be identified by name, fearing what he calls the Somali government's "sensitivity" to sharks, "because people come running to the beach from all directions."

SHARK ATTACKS aside, there is precious little running, brisk walking or expeditious movement of any kind in this steaming city on the Indian Ocean. Somalis here have perfected a deliberate, dignified pace that allows them to stroll the crumbling, sand-swept streets of this 1,000-year-old city without breaking into a sweat.

Unless one adopts this Mogadishu saunter, one sweats miserably and steps on the (often bare) heels of the locals. There is little point, anyway, in rushing around this town of 1 million people. For when one arrives on time for an appointment, the object of that appointment often is not in.

The workday begins, allegedly, at 7 a.m. and ends at 3 p.m., when offices close and everyone saunters home for a nap. Many government offices, however, are empty all day, as evidenced by endlessly ringing telephones.

Behind this ringing emptiness stands the abysmal pay scale of Somali civil servants. They have not had a pay raise in 26 years. Department heads earn only $30 a month, barely enough to feed a family of four here for a week. Many civil servants, therefore, have outside business interests. And, since Mogadishu sleeps in the afternoon, these bureaucrat-entrepreneurs would go broke if they did not take care of business by ducking out on jobs in the morning.

"IT IS ONE of the odd characteristics of the climate . . . that it is practically impossible to remain both immobile and conscious."

Evelyn Waugh wrote this a half century ago of Aden, a city north of here on the southern tip of the Saudi Arabian peninsula. But the observation fits contemporary Mogadishu.

In the city's central market, a sandy, fly-infested sprawl of goat carcasses, cassette tapes, ravishing Somali woman and great mounds of overripe bananas, infectious somnolence lurks behind every tea stall.

Market teamsters, who drive donkey carts into the city at dawn, sack out on the empty beds of their carts as soon as they have unloaded the day's haul of mangoes or mutton. They snore contentedly as their donkeys, still in harness, stand immobile, slowly blinking their long eyelashes in the ferocious morning sunlight.

Afternoon finds shoe-shine boys asleep on shady sidewalks, their heads resting on piles of brushes, shoe polish and rags. Polio cripples, their spiny legs splayed beneath them, sleep, too, on the sidewalks. At the Mogadishu duty-free shop, which only opens in the afternoon and only sells to customers with foreign passports, the music on the store's stereo is Dave Brubeck's "Take Five."

Even when Mogadishu is mobile and conscious, the city's routine business is performed adagio. Consider, for instance, the cashing of a traveler's check.

I attempted this transaction at 8 a.m. at Mogadishu's largest financial institution, the Central Bank of Somalia. At the sight of my check, a clerk slowly turned away from the foreign exchange counter and commenced a languid and extended search for four sheets of carbon paper. He calmly swiped an ancient adding machine from another clerk's desk. It needed to be plugged in, however. This necessitated a slow-motion wrestling match with the Central Bank's primary power source: A long black extension cord snaking across the center of the bank's marble floor.

After 30 minutes of logistics and calculations, the clerk said, "Go sit on that bench and wait."

How long? Some minutes more. Twenty minutes later, the clerk directed me across the marble floor to teller window number nine. There, behind a bullet-proof window, was a perfectly blank ledger book, no money, no human being.

Ten minutes later, a second clerk walked into the booth, dropped off my traveler's check and, without saying a word, walked away. After 10 more minutes, a third clerk came in and cheerfully gave me my money.

THE CASUAL approach to business in Mogadishu extends also to religion. Wild-eyed Khomeinism and gun-toting Shiitism do not wash in this officially Islamic state. Women on the city's streets wear no veils. Loose-fitting wraps of cotton and silk expose their faces, their arms and a goodly portion of their backs. In 1975, when 10 fundamentalist mullahs protested a new law giving property rights to Somali women, the mullahs were shot. Liquor is sold here every day.

"All of us are nomads or the descendents of nomads. A nomad does not know if tomorrow the water well will dry up or if his goats will be eaten by hyenas. This gives us an instinctively pragmatic approach to life," explains Ibrahim Mohamud Abyan, president of the Somali Institute for Administration, Development and Management.

It does a Somali no good, Abyan says, to be a fanatic.

It is, therefore, nomadic fatalism, not Islamic fanaticism, that explains why teen-age Somali soccer players continue to cool off in the late afternoons by swimming naked among the sharks.

One evening, just before sunset, I watched them play soccer and swim in the sea. Fatalistic or not, they approached the surf skittishly and no one stayed in the water very long.

— Blaine Harden

SUMMARY OF HISTORY

SUMMARY OF SOMALI HISTORY

Pharaonic Era	Egyptians traded for frankincense and myrrh and recorded accounts of the people of the "Land of Punt" which was northern Somalia.
60 A.D.	A Greek travel guide to the Indian Ocean indicated substantial trade between the Arabian Peninsula and East African coast.
6th Century	Existence of Mogadishu evidenced by links to Arabian Peninsula.
7th Century	Influx of immigrants from sheikhdoms along the Red Sea spread Islam through the Horn of Africa.
9th Century	Chinese documented trade in the Horn of Africa at Berbera.
10th Century	Merchants from Arabian Peninsula established posts in Brava and Merca, south of Mogadishu.
12th Century	Influx of Persian trade activity in Mogadishu.
1331	Moroccan traveler, Ibn Battuta, reported Mogadishu to be a prosperous trade center.
15th Century	The legendary Adjuran clan confederation ruled the riverine regions of southern Somalia.
1506	The Portuguese bombarded Brava.
1507	Ahmed Gurey, Somalia's first national hero, drove the invading Portuguese from Somalia.
1540	Ahmed Gurey lead a successful invasion into Abyssinia.
1542	Ahmed Gurey defeated in battle near Lake Tana.
18th Century	Inhabitants of Lower Shabelle and Juba River Valley defeat the Adjuran who have since been an enigmatic clan skattered throughout East Africa.
1827	Britain signed treaty with the Somali clan in Berbera.
1828	Mogadishu bombarded and sacked by Omani fleet.
1838	Mogadishu divided as result of a feud between inhabitants of Shingani and Hamarweyn sections of the town.
1854	Richard Burton traveled through Somalia and wrote about the pervasiveness of Somali poetry.
1859	France signed a treaty with the Somalis in what will be known as Djibouti.
1870-90	Menelik II, Emperor of Abyssinia, expanded his control into the Ogaden.
1880	Mogadishu became involved in trade agreements with the Europeans.
1884	Britain signed treaty of protection with the Somali clans along the Gulf of Aden coast.
1900	Said Mohamed Abdille Hassan (the Mad Mullah) and his dervishes began a 20 year, holy jihad against the British colonialists.
1905	Italy established trade dominance on the southern coast of Somalia and designated Mogadishu as a colonial capital.
1920	British defeated Said Mohamed at Taleh ending his jihad.
1925	Italy added the Juba River Valley to its sphere of influence.
1935	Mussolini invaded Ethiopia from Somalia.
1941	British liberated Ethiopia and returned Ogaden to Ethiopian control.
1947	Somali Youth League formed. The SYL became a dominant political force up to and beyond independence.
1950	Italian U.N. trusteeship territory established in southern Somalia after World War II.

June 26, 1960	British Somaliland achieved independence.
July 1, 1960	Italian Somaliland achieved independence, and the north and south unite to form the Republic of Somalia.
1961 and 64	Somalia failed to gain ground in border skirmishes with Ethiopia over the Ogaden.
October 15, 1969	President Shermake was assasinated.
October 21, 1969	Mohamed Siad Barre seized power in a military coup.
1974-75	Haile Selassie deposed in a Marxist coup in Ethiopia. At same time a drought hit the Ogaden region.
1977-78	Siad Barre launched an attack into Ethiopia and gained control of most of the Ogaden. The Soviets backed the Markist regime in Addis Ababa and, with Soviet arms and the help of Cuban troops, the Ethiopians run the Somali army back across the border.
1988	Insurgents in the northwest, the Somali National Movement, lead assaults on government installations. Siad Barre ordered air attacks on Hargeisa. Hargeisa was destroyed and the SNM was chased into Ethiopia.
1989	Mohamed Farah Aideed, who supported Siad Barre's coup and served as a colonel in the 77-78 war with Ethiopia, joined the guerilla movement in the south.
	Ali Mahdi eluded arrest by Siad Barre for his role in financing and supporting rebel movements.
End of 1990	Ali Mahdi returned to Mogadishu to lead rebel movements in the city.
Jan 1991	Farah Aideed led a well-trained and well-armed rebel force into Mogadishu chasing Siad Barre and his loyalists out of Mogadishu, and eventually, out of Somalia.

Political Map of Somalia

CLAN MAP OF THE ETHNIC GROUPS OF SOMALIA

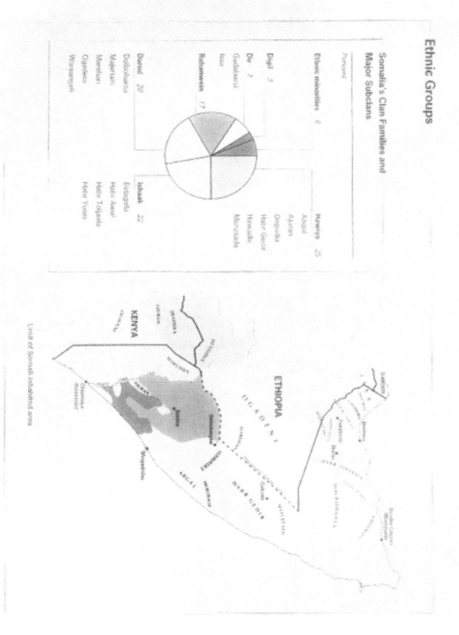

STREET MAP OF MOGADISHU WITH U.S. EMBASSY BUILDINGS

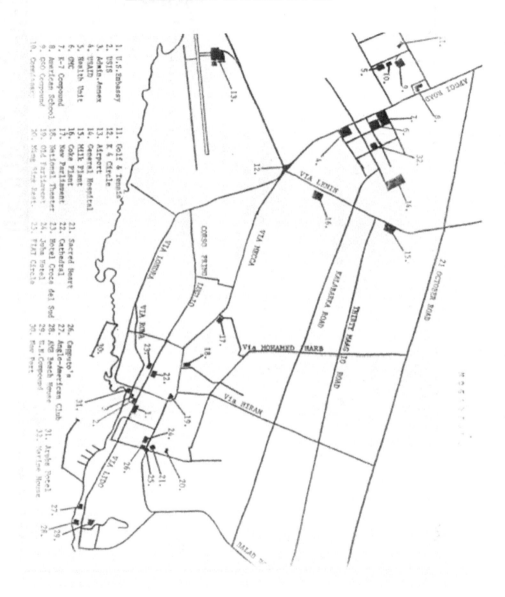

1. U.S.Embassy
2. USIS
3. Admin.Annex
4. USAID
5. Health Unit
6. CMC
7. K-7 Compound
8. American School
9. GSO Compound
10. Commissary

11. Golf & Tennis
12. K & Circle
13. Airport
14. General Hospital
15. Milk Plant
16. Coke Plant
17. New Parliament
18. National Theater
19. Old Parliament
20. King Size Rest.

21. Sacred Heart
22. Cathedral
23. Hotel Croce del Sud
24. Juba Hotel
25. FIAT Circle

26. Cesguto's
27. Anglo-American Club
28. ANB Beach House
29. U.S.Compound
30. Blue Post

31. Atribe Hotel
32. Marine House

MAP OF PAPUA NEW GUINEA

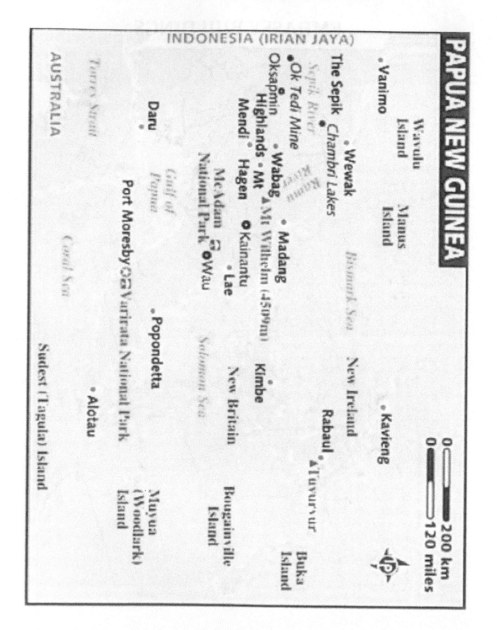

ABOUT THE AUTHORS

Russell Wolford was born in Ohio and graduated from Ohio State University. He worked as a government bureaucrat in pre-war Somalia, a project director building low cost houses in the South Pacific and a country director managing a relief project in war-torn Somalia. He founded a refugee resettlement organization in Ohio during the time of a large influx of refugees from East Africa. He has been in the middle of some tumultuous events and offers honest, first-hand accounts.

Patricia Wolford was born in China to a Foreign Service family. She lived in many places and was familiar with the comfortable lifestyle of embassy personnel. She graduated from UCLA. After marrying Russell and joining him on Third World adventures, she showed that she was a rebel and willing to do the hard work necessary to help the downtrodden and to be an advocate for the underdog. She raised a family, helped juvenile delinquents in a Port Moresby slum and fed street children in Nairobi, Kenya. Her heart for the needy truly shows in her narratives.

Russell and Patricia Wolford in Saakow, Weyn, Somalia